Who Pays Who?

HOW ABUNDANCE CREATED BY ARTIFICIAL INTELLIGENCE WOULD PAY FOR UNIVERSAL BASIC INCOME

Also from R.S. Amblee

The Audacity of Futurism

2017 National Indie Excellence Award

The Ugly Fight: Unleashing AI on Global Warming

Best Book Award Finalist, 2018 American Book Festival

Who Pays Who?

HOW ABUNDANCE CREATED BY ARTIFICIAL INTELLIGENCE WOULD PAY FOR UNIVERSAL BASIC INCOME

R.S. Amblee

GLOTURE BOOKS

ISBN: 9781090448668

In the middle of difficulty lies opportunity.
- Albert Einstein

CONTENTS

Introduction

The Unfathomable Artificial Intelligence

I suppose this book started when I delved deeply into the unfathomable artificial intelligence (AI). The world of AI seemed so grandiose that I was simply lost in it. AI is pretty much in every facet of our businesses: energy, manufacturing, food, healthcare, transportation, and even house construction. Just out of curiosity I began to explore AI's capabilities to take away our jobs in the future, and to my surprise I found many jobs have already eaten up by AI but at an insignificantly small scale. We still have some breathing time before our careers scuffle through a paradigm shift.

Artificial intelligence is one of the more colossal innovations ever conceived by humanity. In many ways AI is a double-edged sword. When we nurture AI to increase our comforts, undoubtedly it will threaten our jobs. And I found AI has amazing potential to foster the unemployed. The unemployed need not be a drag on the economy if we nurture AI in a planned way.

I have done my best to bring all the current global endeavors under one roof giving the AI a form, a shape, and a voice, so the world would recognize its importance and build it strategically. A strategy that builds societal abundance to foster its victims.

Chapter 1

Men Not at Work

It is estimated that more than four million taxi and truck drivers will lose their jobs if autonomous cars become ubiquitous. That technology is just around the corner. The world is set to embrace it without giving a second thought about the consequences of this technology. Or should they? For most of the population, self-driving is a big relief. It is assuredly much cheaper to board an autonomous taxi than a taxi with a driver. It's a no-brainer to imagine most driving jobs would be under threat.

With online sales going thru the roof, the retail apocalypse has finally descended upon the United States. Isn't it more comfortable to order online than going into crowded stores? With a few mouse clicks, your product will be at your doorstep in a couple of days, and even that could shrink to few hours in the near future with Amazon's plans to utilize drones, automated vehicles, and robots, all managed with efficient logistics. Many retail brick-and-mortar stores are already pulling their shutters down as they can't compete with e-commerce. Brace for this, ladies and gentlemen; there were more than fifteen million people working in the retail industry as of 2018. Not all jobs will go away, but most will.

It is also feared that almost ten million jobs will disappear in the construction industry if 3-D printed homes hit the market. China is already building livable homes using 3-D printers. A printer can build a five-hundred-square-feet house in twenty-four hours for less than $10,000, which would normally cost $50,000 or more if manually built. This is the price tag before the mass production of 3-D printers. As the market blossoms, the price will further plummet. A few networked printers could print a large, luxury home in one day. A $1 million home could be built for 20 percent or less. Three-D technology is set to destroy the traditional construction industry.

Manufacturing, agricultural, tourism, hotels, restaurants, transportation—pretty much every industry will soon be affected by technology. What a mess we are going to witness.

Advanced technologies are often called disruptive technologies. That's what their nature is. They disrupt traditional careers and traditional businesses, shaking the very status quo.

Disruptive technologies are not meant to destroy jobs. They are meant to improve our standard of living. Job loss is inevitable collateral damage. Disruptive technologies emphatically create new jobs, new careers, and a whole new world.

Twenty years ago few imagined that Google would one day be a multinational company. Today the company has well over sixty thousand employees globally. Companies like Amazon, Apple, Microsoft, and Facebook have created millions of jobs directly or indirectly. People realized the demand for high-tech jobs, got trained, acquired skills, and became the backbone of these companies, building new careers. Universities too have evolved new curriculums. Much of this has happened over the past two decades. It's been a massive transformation indeed.

However, now the worry is not just the archetypal technological growth but its rapid growth because of the arrival of artificial intelligence (AI).

It is appropriate at this time to draw a distinction between disruptive technologies and AI. The disruptive technologies like 3-D printing, autonomous cars, online shopping, drone delivery of goods, and a zillion others are popping up all over the globe in a very short period of time.

They are definitely not accidental inventions. You may wonder why now. The most likely answer is computer speed. As it increases the technologies evolve faster. These faster computers also gave birth to AI. In fact AI is not a new invention at all. As noted earlier the concept was sitting on the back burners for decades as computers were very slow. Now with faster computers, all AI concepts that were on white papers are now flooding the market at an appropriate time. Good or bad, disruptive technologies and AI are both evolving at the same time. However, the grave concern is that AI is now further disrupting every other disruptive technology.

This rapid growth in technologies that are influenced by AI has people worried whether they have enough time to jack up their skillsets to go back to work like they always did in the past.

What about those who get left behind in the job market, the modern-day versions of blacksmiths and horse-carriage drivers? The word that comes to our mind is humanitarianism. The truth is we could feed the unemployed only if we have abundance. It is not just a one-time donation. It's a long-term commitment to support a huge population of unemployed consistently without inflicting a wound on the growing economy.

If we build an opulent society then yes, the basic needs of human beings—housing, transportation, food, and healthcare—can be provided. The nation can take care of the unemployed and the poor if there is abundance in at least these four areas. There are already social movements demanding some sort of basic income for the poor and unemployed. Global Think Tank is actively deliberating a universal basic income (UBI) for those left behind. No matter how much we debate, this can only be achieved if there is abundance. With the current high cost of living, the UBI is impractical for the huge unemployed population we are forestalling. Any technological development that increases the costs of these necessities is a disaster for UBI. And that is exactly what is happening today.

This book identifies with practical examples how we could nurture AI in these four, critical areas and make them affordable so UBI becomes a possibility. When we nurture artificial intelligence (AI) to enhance our lifestyle and improve our comforts, undoubtedly it will whisk away our jobs. However if we nurture AI strategically, it is possible to survive this massive collateral damage. It is indeed a bitter-sweet indulgence.

Chapter 2

What is AI Anyway?

Artificial intelligence(AI): the intelligence exhibited by self-learning computer software. It is also the name of the academic field of study that is becoming mainstream and has a career path.

This chapter introduces you to AI and its practical applications in the real world with exiting examples. The subsequent chapters detail how AI could be harnessed to feed for unemployed people.

The term artificial intelligence has really fascinated the world. While humans are still early in understanding human intelligence, they have the audacity to build an artificial intelligence.

Being in the IT industry myself for more than two decades, my fascination with this new software kept growing as it became more widespread every day. It's just unbelievable that this weird term that made its academic appearance recently already has a career path in its name. I began to wonder if all the hype was unwarranted or if it AI had true value. I started my own reconnoiter out of unquenchable curiosity. The more I dug, the more captivating I found it.

When it comes to understanding computer programs, there is nothing equivalent to wetting our hands. So I started to learn AI by coding it. I coded a self-driving virtual car that sniffs around and finds its way to the destination with the shortest route. After all the hard work and finally completing the python code, a small, ant-like bug began to crawl on my computer screen, going all over in random directions. That was my AI algorithm.

It crawled all around because the start and end positions were not specified yet. Amazingly, when I keyed in the start and end positions, this little creature slowly changed its course, and instead of moving randomly it began to move around the starting position for a while and then it crawled toward the end position. Once it reached the end position, after maybe ten or fifteen back and forth movements, it learned the quickest way to move between those two points. However, even though it found the shortest way to reach the destination it did not give up its habit of sniffing around to find potential shorter routes to eliminate any possibility of taking a longer route.

That constant sniffing gives AI the special ability to learn from its own mistakes just like humans do. It was just an incredible experience. It's not a typical software that obediently follows the hard rules; this was an ever-learning software. What was moving like an ant all around the screen now began to look more like a commuter car between downtown and the airport—software learning on its own. In my career as an IT professional, I am used to commanding software to do tasks for a specific result. I had never written software that could act on its own to achieve a specific result. It changed my perception of AI forever. So I started learning more about this amazing human creation.

You may be wondering how this software learned the shortest route. The simplest explanation is, it's coded in such a way that the behavior of the bug is dependent on what is called a reward point. Every time the bug moves closer to the destination, it gets a reward point. Every time the bug moves away from the destination, it loses a point. The goal of this computer program is to bag as many rewards as possible.

How does it know which way it has to move to get closer without GPS or any direction sensor? It uses a heuristic computing technique— essentially trial and error—to compute the distance. Every time it moves it computes the distance. That data is then automatically stored in a memory matrix. That's why it initially goes in random directions for a while before finally computing the most optimal way. This computation of an optimal path is called training for the AI, a process that is highly CPU intensive. This unique learning capability is the reason AI is becoming so powerful and the darling of the world.

This heuristic method is not the only technique used in AI. There are tons of them, and they are not new. These are age-old ideas and mathematical models that were never tested on computers because they were dead-slow in previous decades. Now with faster computers, it's no surprise old concepts are being rediscovered.

Another popular AI technique is called artificial neural networks or simply neural net (NN). This is one of the top-notch techniques modeled after the neural structure of the human brain. The disparity is that NN might use a few hundred neurons, whereas the neural structure of the human brain has approximately one hundred billion neurons. It's obvious that humans have a better capability with things like face, object, voice, and natural language recognition as well as many more complex qualities that machines don't have yet. However, NN has the capability to outpace human neural networks very quickly as it takes only a few more central processing units (CPUs)—popularly called chips—and few more gigabits of memory to add more neurons. The truth is the capability of NN is boundless.

Now let's look at the structure of a human neural network a bit more closely from the perspective of data flow. In human brains every neuron is connected to a bunch of other neurons. Obviously, the output of one neuron becomes the input to other neurons, meaning the signal coming from one neuron is captured by other neurons connected to it as their source of information. Based on multiple inputs, a neuron generates a new output that can be used again as input to other neurons. This goes on like a crazy maze in these one hundred billion neurons.

The basic idea here is the strength of input signals decides the output signal from a neuron. If a neuron is getting high-strength signals from all its inputs, its output will be influenced by the strong signals. If you touch a hot plate by accident, all the nerve endings on the hand will send out strong signals to the brain, which cause the brain to act, and your hand is pulled back as a reflex action almost before you are aware of it. The brain processes the inputs and acts on them based purely on the strength or weakness of the signals. The same technique has been adapted in NN. Furthermore, each artificial neuron is designed to use a mathematical function to determine its own output that gives it the ability to recognize objects.

Here is an example of the object recognition capability of NN. Let's say you have a basket of random objects and you want AI to recognize them. In reality NN doesn't know a thing about any object in the basket. It means that the AI has to be trained first. Let's see how we can train AI to recognize a bird say for example. When you show AI an object like a toy bird, the camera image of the bird is broken by the NN into several individual images. Each image is fed to a different neuron that gives its own weight to the image based on its own embedded function.

Some of these images could be very prominent features for identification, while others may not be. For instance, the beak is a prominent feature to identify a bird. As NN are not initially aware of these prominent features, it gives them random weight. Discernibly, the prediction would be random too. If the prediction is incorrect, then weights are readjusted. This happens over and over again until the NN learn all the features that are useful for identification. It will eventually determine which features of the bird are more prominent. The more you train NN, the closer they get to the right answer. For the training we need to use as many varieties of birds as possible.

After training, when a toy or a photo of a bird is shown, the NN will give its best answer. The accuracy of the answer depends on the volume and variations of the data that was fed during training. In other words the quality of data matters. If there is a weird bird that is confusing to the human eye, AI might also falter if it not fed in during the training.

Now if you show the image of an elephant to the bird-trained AI, obviously it will give the wrong answer or no answer at all, as it is untrained to recognize elephants. You can't possibly train AI on every species. This is where big data comes in. If the information about an animal is available in a database, fully identified and tagged, then the AI can skim thru the database and learn from it instantly.

Predictive Capability of AI

Every min about three million messages are posted on Facebook, fifty thousand pictures are shared, half a million tweets tweet out, and forty million texts zip out. Every time we shop, we spawn tons of data tied to banks, retailers, and industries. This mountain of data is given a name:

big data. The blast of big data is so huge it is humanly impossible even for professionals to make sense of it. This level of complexity and volume of data gave birth to software like data analytics tools that extract, analyze, and interpret data in a way that is useful to us.

However, no matter how sophisticated the data analytics software is, it has limited capability and will only do exactly what it is coded for. Big data has innumerable data patterns hidden in it, and it's not possible to code software to unearth all the individual combinations. This was when AI emerged as a natural solution to pull meaningful information out of big data. AI can identify observable patterns and predict things without having explicit pre-programmed rules and models.

For example, if you want to know what city has more crime, a simple database query can figure it out, or a simple data analytics tool can answer that instantly. However, if you want to know what specific locality is going to get hit by a criminal gang in the next twenty-four hours, you have to go thru numerous data sources such as Facebook postings, tweets, texts, Google searches, local demographics, and criminal reports—zillions of data points. It would be humanly impossible to concoct all these structured and unstructured data and predict a pattern of criminal acts. It would be like looking for a needle in a haystack. You need an AI that correlates this massive data in a useful way.

To do the prediction AI has to be trained first. AI is made to predict some past events that have already occurred based on past data. If it makes a mistake, it reevaluates and predicts again, learning iteratively over and over again until it becomes a useful tool. How well AI predicts depends on the quality of data. Garbage in, garbage out is appropriate here. The quality of big data is as important as skillfully coded AI itself. If you want AI to predict anything, the data has to be vast, varied, high-quality, and as real-time as feasible.

The Sources of Big Data

Broadly speaking, there are two kinds of data sources: human generated and machine-generated. Human-generated data includes social media, blogs, Google search, texting, tweeting, online shopping, and so on. Though these data sources appear humungous, they eventually flatten out because data caused by human activity can't be infinite as humans can only do finite things in a day. The data growth seems mammoth because more and more people are gaining access to the Internet every day, and once all seven billion people on the planet become part of the global digital community, we will have reached a level of stability in data generation.

The only data that will continue to grow unabated is machine data. Machines are slowly mushrooming all around us and are expected to grow faster as the economy expands. Every machine generates tons of valuable information. Machines generate useful data via the Internet of Things. Not only are the numbers of machines increasing, but the number of Internet of Things is also increasing, making the future machines highly data-intensive.

What Is the Internet of Things?

Internet of Things (IoT) is another fascinating human creation. In today's world any digital device that connects to the Internet is termed a smart device. All smart devices—smart watches, smart garage doors, smart TVs, smart refrigerators—are IoTs. Any gadget can be made smart by giving it the capability to connect to the Internet. A device cannot be an IoT, no matter how sophisticated it is, if it is not able to connect to the Internet. The reason for emphasizing an Internet connection is that it gives the device a unique identity in the digital world. We call this unique ID an Internet Protocol (IP) address. Every computer in the world today has an IP address. That is how we recognize every computer on the planet quickly. An IoT can't connect to the Internet unless it has an IP address. That is an IoT becomes uniquely recognizable in the world.

Examples of the Internet of Things

Say you have a smart refrigerator, which can do many helpful things like inform you when the milk is empty, when the eggs are gone, and so on. These capabilities come from the IoT sensors. The milk sensor of the IoT is set up to know the weight of the milk carton. When you place your milk carton at the designated spot, the sensor will measure the weight of the milk and send the data to the IoT. In essence an IoT is an agent between its sensors and the Internet. A more apt definition is that an IoT is a smart chip that constantly captures data via its sensors and sends it to the Internet. Once the data is on the Internet, an AI can easily pick it up and do analysis on it.

In this smart refrigerator, similarly, the egg sensor sends the weight of the eggs to the IoT. The IoT chip in turn captures and sends out data to the Internet from where your phone app (run by AI) would pick it up. And your phone app will do whatever it is configured to do. Maybe it will beep or send a text or email to you. It may even order milk if you have set it up that way. From this IoT data AI learns your usage pattern and advises you based on how you have configured it.

Today's smart homes are filled with IoTs. From room thermostats all the way to garbage bins there are IoTs. In smart homes AI needs a lot of data to learn and become a useful tool. For instance, if you want AI to prepare coffee when you wake up or to switch off the lights and close the garage when you leave the house or even to start the furnace and keep the house warm before you arrive, AI needs data to learn your lifestyle. IoTs brew mammoth amount of such data for AI in smart homes. While IoT is a data producer AI is a data analyzer. This interdependency is what makes them a powerful duo to bring comfort to our lives.

Here is an invigorating example to show how city administrations could use our home IoTs to save energy. Say it is an exceptionally hot summer day and the power utility company is experiencing blackouts. When customers lose power, the utility staff can spend hours or days fixing the problem and dealing with angry customers. In an IoT world, this can be entirely different. The utility staff could quickly react to avert a blackout by turning everyone's thermostat up five degrees. A good AI could even alert the utility staff to an impending blackout. Or the AI itself could proactively turn thermostats up five degrees at all smart homes and non-essential businesses, leaving temperature-sensitive facilities such as hospitals and refrigerated warehouses alone. IoT and AI can do wonders if they are harnessed efficiently.

Here is a good example of IoT in healthcare. Say a patient is remotely monitored with a wearable device and the heart rate increases to an unsafe level. The IoT senses the data in real-time and transmits it. This data has to be analyzed, and the abnormalities need to be identified. If this responsibility is assigned to an individual who is monitoring patients remotely, reviewing data from thousands of patients in real-time is impossible. Even coding software with rules is time-consuming and fraught with errors. This is where AI comes in. It analyzes data in real time as it gets collected and flags anything outside the norm. This data sharing between AI and IoT is lifesaving.

IoTs around the world are producing a treasure trove of machine data on traffic, weather, crime, healthcare, supermarkets, industrial robotics, smart homes, and so on. AI is taking advantage of big data and is evolving, and its capabilities are all-encompassing: sales projections, crime prediction, weather forecasting, object, face, language, and voice recognition, and even playing chess.

What is RFID?

It is worth discussing radio frequency identification (RFID) as it can send information directly to IoTs. Similar to its sensors, IoTs can grab information from RFID as well. RFID is nothing but a digital barcode. The difference is that in a regular bar code, the data is static; it can't be updated. In an RFID system data can be updated. RFID tags are good for storing vital information like expiration date, manufacturing date, package destination, and so on.

The RFID tags or microchips store all the vital (static) data that can be updated. They can be attached to objects like an automobile during production to track their progress through the assembly line. The RFID-tagged pharmaceutical products are very popular nowadays. RFID tags can even be in used in livestock and pets for their identification and tracking.

As RFID tags do not have the capability to connect to the Internet, they have very little value without a reading device called RFID reader. To understand the usefulness of RFID, let's take the example of the smart refrigerator again. Say you bought a carton of milk with an RFID tag and stored it in your smart refrigerator. The RFID reader in the refrigerator reads the tag and sends its expiration date to the IoT in the refrigerator which in turn sends it to the Internet. However, RFID can't sense the weight of the milk carton and hence can't send dynamic information about how much milk is still left in the carton. RFID can only give static data and not dynamic data as it is not a sensor.

RFID existed well before IoTs came into the market. They are gaining more importance in today's logistic world because they feed vital data to IoTs that forwards the data to the Internet where it becomes more useful.

RFIDs can cost anywhere from a few cents to several dollars depending on the size and range of data transmittal. They can be as small as postage stamps or as big as your car transponder. RFID usage is quite widespread in credit cards, hotel room cards, car keys, car transponders, passports, ID cards, driver license cards—they are pretty much everywhere.

RFID reader can simultaneously read several hundred tags. The RFID reader can hang from the ceiling and read all the tags in a warehouse and send the inventory list to the connected IoT. As RFIDs are not connected to the Internet, an IoT makes an RFID come to life.

RFID technology is very useful in warehouses to track inventory. Even trucks are attached with RFID. As they go from one warehouse to another, they are read and tracked. Many cars have RFID transponders that can be used in tollways and parking lots to open the gates. Any object can be tagged with RFID: key chains, wallets, bicycles, pets, and even hospital patients. RFID is very useful in pharmacies to manage inventory. Soon you will see express checkouts where your shopping cart is instantly scanned eliminating customers having to hand scan items.

Data security is a major issue as RFID can give out our secrets. Say you bought an expensive Rolex watch; the RFID tag on the watch could be broadcasting it as you walk down the street. A smart thief can figure it out. These kinds of security issues are being ironed out.

There are also some technical problems to address. Since RFID uses radio frequencies, it can jam when using overlapping frequencies. This could be life-threatening in a hospital. RFID readers are prone to collision issues when signals overlap. However, anti-collision protocols are being developed to counter that. The bottom line is technical challenges are not showstoppers; they only make the system better. Amid all the technical limitations, RFID has become an extended arm for IoTs to capture data.

The take away from this discussion is that IoTs and RFID are like eyes or ears for AI to make decisions. Whenever you hear the words big data, remember IoTs and RFID is where most, if not all, of the machine data will be coming from.

Amazon Go, the innovative new shopping technology is going one step ahead. It uses a different kind of technology to capture data and send it to the AI for analysis. Each Amazon Go store is fitted with hundreds of cameras that track items customers put in their bags, then add the item to their online shopping cart. If the customer puts the item back onto the shelf, it's removed from their virtual basket. Customers can shop and leave the store without having to stop and pay. When they leave the store, their chosen payment method is charged. All the data captured by the cameras and sensors is sent to AI to process, analyze and predict shopping behavior of the customers.

Now let's explore some interesting AI applications we have in the market today. With each of these examples, give your best thoughts to diagnose what jobs might disappear and what new opportunities could pop up and what skills we may need to grab them early on.

AI in Movies

The entertainment industry is going to hit $800 billion soon. It's a massive industry and is undoubtedly attracting AI to streamline the movie-making process to give audiences more bang for their buck.

Recently a movie trailer was produced by AI. IBM Watson (AI software) created a ten-minute trailer for the movie *Morgan*. Watson went through the movie and selected a few emotional movements of love, hate, anger, and horror then made a few short clippings for the director to choose from. (To see the *Morgan* trailer, Google it; enthralling to watch.) AI not only saved millions of dollars, but it also introduced its own machine ideas, surprising even the creators of AI, which is still bad at reading human emotion but is getting better.

Similar attempts are going on in Japan. McCann Erickson Japan introduced a new AI "creative director" named AI-CD ß that made a commercial for Clorets mints. The AI was given a decade's worth of commercial ads to learn from. Though AI has not been fully established in the film industry, it's at the doorstep. (To see its ad, Google AI-CD beta.)

AI in Sports

IBM Watson has entered Wimbledon. Its video software uses crowd noise, social traction, facial recognition, and sentiment analysis of players to generate automated video highlights. So a video editor will no longer need to cut and edit to put a highlights package together.

AI in Chatbots

Chances are you already have some sort of chatty virtual assistant or chatbot: Alexa, SIRI, GoogleNow, Cortana, and so on. Amazon's Alexa sits inside each Echo speaker. It can play your favorite music, announce the day's weather and so on. It can even order items online and control home devices if it is configured that way. The goal of this AI is to learn your daily habits and give you a helping hand to make life litter easier. These chatbots listen to you, observes your behavior, learn about you every time you tweet, watch a movie, listen to music, conduct Google searches, and make online purchases. As it learns, it serves more efficiently. This may look more like an invasion of privacy, but that is what the world chose.

As these devices learn a lot about us, they become gold mines for hackers. Many are seriously concerned about their private data being stolen by some unscrupulous. Security issues have put a damper on the growth of this technology to some extent. Nonetheless, the demand for such devices is increasing.

Similarly, Apple's SIRI runs on iPhones and understands multiple ways of asking questions, so you don't need to worry about remembering exact phrasing for commands. Google Now in Android systems knows your commute, your interests, and details about your daily schedule. It is loaded with predictive features. Microsoft's Cortana is great for location-based reminders. Most e-commerce websites nowadays are chat enabled.

Companies train these chatbots—literally chat robots—before putting them live for customers to use. During training they use most frequently used questions and relevant answers creating an answer bank. However, if the question that a customer asks is outside of the answer bank, then it will either give an irrelevant answer or a totally wrong answer. However, if they are AI-assisted, then they would learn every time you chat with them.

Here is a simple litmus test to see if the chatbot that claims to be AI really is or not. Ask the virtual assistant some sample questions and note the responses. If you repeatedly ask these questions over a certain period of time, maybe a few weeks or months, and the answer is the same, most probably it is not yet using AI. On the other hand, if this gadget is learning about you and is giving you a more useful response each time, then in all probability it could be using some sort of AI and is capturing your personal data.

Two-Day Product Delivery

Major retailers do purchase prediction. Most of the time when you browse for a product, the AI in their websites identify you as a potential customer and email you special offers. They can send you coupons, offer you discounts, and target you with advertisements while also stocking their warehouses that are close to you with products that you're likely to buy. That is how your product is delivered the next day.

Product delivery is becoming smarter and beginning to look more like fire stations servicing specific areas. They need to get to the fire within a specific time frame, so stations are strategically located throughout the city. A similar system is being used in product delivery, which is why Amazon has been building warehouses all over the United States. Each warehouse services a specific area, and the AI knows the needs of that population, so each warehouse is uniquely stocked to cater to a specific demographic population. Likewise, when customers browse for products online, AI knows which products will be in the greatest demand during the coming holiday season and stocks accordingly. All these decisions need a lot of data and analytics in real-time done every min of the day. AI is built to make these decisions and constantly learn from its mistakes.

AI in Humanoids

The robot Sophia is a social humanoid created by Hong Kong-based Hanson Robotics. Sophia was activated on April 19, 2015. This robot imitates human gestures and facial expressions. It can answer questions on certain predefined topics. Sophia was designed to be a conversational companion for people in retirement communities, hospitals, and nursing homes. It is also capable of entertaining crowds thru social conversation. This humanoid is on YouTube, and it's captivating to watch the facial expressions on this robot.

The AI algorithm was designed by SingularityNET, which aims to foster an open market for AIs.

AI in Policing

The American company ShotSpotter has developed a technology to help identify gunshots. It has placed sensors in most tall buildings in cities, and when a gun is fired, these sensors capture the sound and vibrations and mutually exchange data to pinpoint the exact location of the gunshot and alert the police. This is not only saving lives but also reducing the time and effort to respond, eventually reducing the cost.

Another interesting twist comes from a US company called Predpol which can detect crime before it happens. They look at history and figure out the crime trend and identify potential areas and possible time of day. Though they can't predict the exact location or exact time, their predictions would help police be on alert during a specified window of time, which would potentially save lives, time, and money.

The Chinese company Hikvision uses video surveillance cameras to read license plates, use facial recognition, and even detect unattended bags in crowded areas and alert law enforcement officers.

Another Chinese company, Cloud Walk, is going one step ahead. It is using facial recognition software to identify suspicious and unusual body language that could trigger a security alert. Machines are not only learning but saving data on those individuals to help AI evolve to counter crime.

AI in Recruiting

Are you looking for a job right now or likely to look for one in the near future? Chances are you will be interacting with a virtual assistant most likely driven by AI. This AI may concern you because it learns a lot about you and stores all that data digitally, so your profile will be available to all potential employers.

Employers should also be equally concerned as their profile will also be available to all potential candidates. If the employer is racially biased, it will show up in the recruitment history.

You can't avoid this route. So be prepared to face this digital challenge and be attentive to what you give out. Since you will be interfacing with a machine instead of a human, it could be a new experience. You may ask the wrong questions or give the wrong answers to AI. Everything is digitally recorded.

One fascinating thing that has happened to the recruitment process is that biases are slowly being extinguished. The AI software scans through the résumés of potential candidates without considering gender, age, and name to eliminate biases that could steer the focus away from promising candidates. It also flags missing information from the résumés that the employer is looking for.

When candidates apply for a job, even before the résumés reaches the employer, AI-driven software will communicate with candidates not only to collect more information and do prescreening tests but also to share employer information. This helps the candidates as well by knowing if they are looking at the right employer before attending any further face-to-face interviews to avoid wasting time for both. Employers love this approach. Remember; the fundamental approach has not changed. To effectively prescreen the candidates, AI asks challenging questions and looks for effective answers.

Many recruiting AIs are becoming proactive and going one step further in compiling a list of potential candidates not currently in the job market but who may seek employment in the future. AI can identify which candidate would be likely to change jobs because of a company merger or layoffs. Also if a candidate updates their LinkedIn profile, it's a sign that the candidate could be looking for a new job.

Hiring is now popularly referred to as talent acquisition. There are plenty of talent acquisition companies like LinkedIn, Indeed, Glassdoor, Dice, Monster, Craigslist, Plaxo, Jobster, and so on. There are also many companies that are developing talent acquisition software like Ideal, Avrio, Entelo, Engage Talent, Paradox Olivia, and Mya Systems. You may visit their sites to learn how they are developing and using

AI to acquire talent. These companies focus on developing machine learning software to mediate between candidates and employers.

AI in the Stock Market

Picking promising stocks every day is arduous for portfolio managers and needs a lot of proficient people. They have to scan data coming from news media, social media, blogs, company announcements, consumer confidence reports, real-time volatility in the stock market, etc. The amount of data is so exhaustive it is implausible to analyze and arrive at fortune stocks to invest in. This is where machine learning is picking up steam.

The US company Kavout is engaged in building deep learning algorithms to assist individuals in trading. People can now hire AI instead of humans for trading.

This company also uses sentiment analysis, which looks at how people, traders, investors, company CEOs, and others react to any stock market news. AI is using all this data to make good investment decisions.

AI is also influencing algorithmic trading and high-frequency trading systems. Many robot advisors are in the market today. Most hedge funds and financial institutions have their own version of AI.

As you can see the data is so vast and varied, that the AIs of different companies analyze them in different ways. So there is competition to build the best AI for the stock market. The race is on; the winners are the individuals like us. Skilled jobs are plenty in this ever-inflating financial industry.

AI still needs babysitting in many ways, as any software glitch could wipe out portfolios. The computer glitch of 2012 has left a bad taste in everyone's mouth. Although AI is threatening the traditional portfolio management jobs, the financial market still needs people who can understand both AI and business at the same time. Portfolio managers have to learn to live with AI, which offers both a job threat and job opportunities at the same time.

AI in Rescue Operations

Do you know there are unique robots that look like and act like animals? For example, eMotion Butterflies from the company Festo fly like real ones. Their dragonfly-like BionicOpter robots fly and glide in the air. Their bionic ants are the size of a hand. Their AquaPenguin can swim in water, look, and act like real penguins. Their bionic kangaroo looks like and jumps like a real kangaroo. There are captivating videos online that are worth watching.

The Defense Advanced Research Projects Agency (DARPA), a wing of the US Department of Defense, has created a variety of incredible robots. It's riveting to watch these robots in action on YouTube videos.

These amazing machines are a blessing in disguise for disaster response. They can fly, crawl, or walk into places humans can't. They can operate in environments where humans can't even survive. During disasters like hurricanes, tornadoes, floods, forest fires, nuclear leakages, and earthquakes they bring data of immense value. While some of them can collect data others can help in real rescue operations.

Future rescue is all about AI-driven intelligent, quick-witted, canny robots. Though AI is being blamed for taking away our jobs, if you look at the quality of services it is providing and how much value it is adding to society, we can only cherish the technology.

AI in Robotics

Regrettably, robots have a very limited number of sensors, so a very limited amount of data is fed to the robot brain. Most of the robotic movements are hard coded using limited incoming data. No wonder robots are very limited in their capability. Compare this to the human body. For instance, the skin that covers the human body is filled with trillions of nerve endings. You touch the skin with a needle, and you will not find one single area that can't sense it unless you have a skin disease.

Now imagine filling the robotic body with such a vast number of sensors, generating a prodigious amount of data at a staggering rate. No hard-coded software can handle such a mammoth amount of data. You need a brain that is capable of analyzing the data to maneuver the robotic movement efficiently. This is probably the reason for such slow development in robotic technology. It took years for engineers to make a robot walk. They were struggling to hard code the rules with scanty data. Now with the arrival of AI and affordable IoTs, hard coding is fading away. Robots are evolving noticeably faster. In fact we see new versions of them every year. This is giving a big boost to the manufacturing industry.

AI in Drones

In a captivating TED Talk worth watching, Professor Vijay Kumar from the University of Pennsylvania demonstrated tiny drones (flying robots) performing a series of intricate maneuvers, flying through confined spaces without colliding or interfering with each other. These smart drones are capable of aiding in construction, shipping, and even responding to emergencies.

AI in Weather Forecasting

Have you heard of hindcasting? With AI there is no forecasting without hindcasting. Climate models that are currently out there today were first trained with historical data, and the predicted values are compared with actual past events. Historical records that date back thousands of years can help AI developers build predictive models.

Many global companies are keeping aggressive development in these critical areas. The Weather Company, an IBM Business, announced its plans to focus on a project called Deep Thunder that can train machine learning models to predict the impact of weather.

Panasonic is another company that is deep into improving weather technology. It recently purchased AirDat that makes a popular sensor called TAMDAR that can be installed on aircraft. It has started a similar global forecasting system called Panasonic Global 4-D which predicted Hurricane Irma more accurately than other models.

Threats to AI

Before wrapping up this chapter, let's look at the technological threats facing AI. There are two broad categories of AI. The first is a hard-coded slave category that mimics only human actions. This category has many names: basic AI, reactive AI, weak AI, or narrow AI (ANI).

The second category is widely called general purpose AI or AGI. This can learn and improve over time, a kind of self-learning. Most AIs that we have today are hybrids with both rigid ANI features and some AGI learning capability.

We shouldn't get too bogged down with these academic terminologies of AI classifications, but there is a strong reason we need to know the distinction. Some AI experts think that it could be dangerous that we still have many rigid ANIs that are not learning from its mistakes. Anyone can hack ANI to knock out our electric grid, damage nuclear power plants, and misdirect robots causing global-scale economic damages.

There is an urgent need to develop smart self-learning AIs that we all can depend on. For now we have to be on constant vigil to protect ANIs from outside attacks. We shouldn't get too excited if some utility company adopts an AI. If it's more of a basic ANI with little or no self-learning capability, it could be doing more harm than good as it can't figure out the attackers. It is better that we understand this AI categorization, so we know the threats we are facing.

Most AI software is proprietary, which means we don't know how they are coded. The AI coded by Google may be entirely different from AI coded by Facebook or Amazon. Aptly, open source is beginning to take shape to exchange AI codes and its faster evolution.

Until ANI evolves to a safe zone, there will be a great demand for anti-viruses to thwart ANI hackers. These are the areas of new opportunities. There is also an effort to build a library of ANI talents to quickly evolve ANI. As this library sprouts and the open AI platform widens globally, future opportunities in the AI world would be unprecedented.

Careers in AI

As explored in the previous chapter while more than half the current United States workforce will be at risk in the next decade or so, a plethora of new jobs will be in AI-related fields.

AI uses many machine learning techniques such as heuristic, deep Q-learning, reinforcement learning, neural networks, and so on. Most AI systems are written in Python and R languages, although AI can be coded in any language. In the future as more powerful languages are introduced, programmers would make that shift.

The most prudent way to insulate your career is to learn automation related subjects like programming, hardware, big data storage, big data analytics, cybersecurity, cloud networking or any subset of data-science discipline that may interest you. Even if your career is nothing to do with Information Technology like those of physicians, lawyers or even artists must make an attempt to understand this new filed as it is going to threaten everyone's job in the very near future. If you are considering learning AI just for academic interest, there are many courses available online. The earlier you start learning, the better it is. It is very hard to learn those fundamental concepts as we grow older, so it would be highly beneficial if these subjects are introduced at elementary school level itself. Such a shift in our education system would surely go a long way in protecting our careers. Those who are starting new careers shouldn't ignore AI.

I hope this chapter gave a glimpse of AI and its current competencies. In the upcoming chapters we will deliberate with practical examples how we could nurture AI predominantly in four areas—housing, transportation, food, and healthcare—and make them affordable, so UBI becomes a possibility for the victims of technological disruption.

Chapter 3

Print a Roof Overhead

This chapter explores how AI would threaten construction jobs and at the same time substantially brings down the cost of construction boosting the economic growth so the unemployment that stems out of its disruption could be easily contained.

Will the world's next megacity splash out of a 3-D printer? Imagine printing a city with the click of a mouse. That is where the 3-D technology is heading. The Dubai-based company Cazza is currently planning to build the world's first 3-D-printed skyscraper in Dubai by 2023. It is committed to supporting the emirate's vision to 3-D-print 25 percent of all of its buildings by 2030.

What is a 3-D printer anyway? Imagine your printer has very thick ink, and you print the same image over and over on the same piece of paper. The ink would accumulate to give a three-dimensional appearance. The 3-D printers utilize materials such as polymer plastic, wood fiber, cement, or metal filament, depending on the need.

The 3-D printers are an advanced version of your home printer. Three-D printing, also called additive manufacturing, is the process of making three-dimensional solid objects using additive processes, where an object is created by laying down successive layers of material until the entire object is created. Each of these layers can be seen as a thinly sliced horizontal cross-section of the eventual object. It starts with making a virtual design of the object that is to be created. This virtual design is made using a computer-aided design (CAD) software or using a 3-D scanner.

Initially 3-D printers came on the market to create prototypes or samples of proposed items before venturing into expensive mass production. As the technology evolved, many manufacturers especially car companies used 3-D printers to create parts for assembly, particularly certain expensive parts. Now 3-D printers are used in all large manufacturing industries to produce many critical parts reducing the need for inventory and transportation.

After years of talk and development, 3-D printing technology is finally entering the construction industry. China is currently a leading driver of 3-D printed houses and seeing more around the world is looking increasingly promising.

There are many potential benefits. Every year in the United States, four hundred thousand workers are seriously injured or killed doing construction work, according to the Occupational Safety and Health Administration (OSHA). Construction also invariably generates tons of waste including wood, drywall, and roofing materials that are sent to the landfills. And construction contributes significantly to environmentally harmful emissions. Automating the construction process using technologies like 3-D printing saves lives, reduces costs, and is better for the environment.

Cazza is not the only company disrupting the construction industry. The San Francisco-based startup, Apis Cor, built a four-hundred-square-feet house in a Russian town within twenty-four hours for a mere $10,000. The company used a mobile 3-D printer with a nozzle to squeeze out concrete. Then workers manually painted it and installed the roof, wiring, hydro-acoustic, and thermal insulation.

A house is an assembly of individual finished products. However, the main structure is the most expensive to create. That is where 3-D printers are winning. Once the structure is complete, how we finish it varies. We can do away with simple materials or indulge in exotic interiors.

The Dutch firm MX3-D is going in a different route. It is using a combination of metal inert gas welders and robotic arms to print large metal structures faster and cheaper. China-based Winsun has built fully functional office space in Dubai. Massachusetts Institute of Technology students have attempted to build a livable house in California using earthy green materials.

The materials used in 3-D printing vary. In Madrid, Spain, the companies Acciona and D-Shape collaborated to build a pedestrian bridge using micro-reinforced concrete material. In the Philippines, the owner of Manila's Lewis Grand Hotel has 3-D printed an extension using sand and volcanic ash. In Massa Lombarda, Italy, the firm Wasp has built a complete village with 3-D printers, using mud, clay, and plant fibers.

The Italian firm D-shape has built a 1,110 square meter house in Amsterdam that looks like an infinite loop. It could be used for exhibition space. Another company has built a bicycle bridge in Gemert, Netherlands, that features eight individual, reinforced, and pre-stressed concrete pieces assembled together. Yet another company has built a canal house in Amsterdam that is made up of thirteen unique rooms.

The list is growing by the day. In the last five years, 3-D startups have sprung up all over the world. There is a huge entrepreneurial opportunity to grab a piece of this global enterprise. It is amazing to watch YouTube channels to see how these 3-D houses are built worldwide.

AI Intervention

Usage of 3-D printers in construction has created some unease regarding safety. In traditional human-built homes, builders make sure the structure is safe by employing various proven engineering methods. Humans have perfected this technology over many centuries. Now with 3-D printing, that human element is replaced by machines. This is a paradigm shift from traditional construction. Similar to self-driving car technology that is going thru sensor anxiety, the 3-D printed houses are facing structure anxiety.

In 3-D printing, the major challenge is that a small defect in a critical location of the building could lead to a catastrophic collapse of the building. As 3-D printing does not follow the traditional pillar and column architecture, this newly found technology could work well for smaller buildings. However, when it is scaled up to large structures, it faces technological challenges along with fiscal justification. This is what has slowed down the development and implementation of this technology. Now with the arrival of AI, there seems to be a huge jump in achieving that needed safety in buildings.

Remember AI is not a construction technology. It's a software that is immensely capable of processing big data and self-learning. AI makes 3-D buildings much safer by scanning for imperfections in real-time during construction itself. Especially if IoTs are embedded in critical locations of the building, they can provide valuable data in real time. They can measure compressive forces, tensile forces, structural strain, stress distribution, and if any minuscule changes occur it instantly transmit its analysis to the cloud. AI can continue to monitor the stability of the structure with data from IoT's after construction ends, making such buildings more secure than traditionally built structures. Moreover, if the building in question totters, AI learns from its mistake.

Once AI is embraced by the construction businesses, it will start disrupting the current business model by eliminating the need for human engineers and laborers. AI can efficiently maneuver the construction robots and can enhance the nozzle performance by determining the right size and shape, depending on the material used. AI can do this instantly if quality data is fed.

AI can easily boost the speed of construction by deploying robots in the right places and navigating them skillfully. The robot maneuvering needs a huge amount of data that only AI can handle. If humans are assigned to this task, they will take ages hard-coding each robotic movement.

With chemistry and metallurgical big data, AI could even suggest viable alternative materials for the structure to suit the topography. Basically AI becomes the 3-D printers' brain in construction.

There are many 3-D printing companies already using AI technology, such as the London-based startup Daghan Cam Limited. It is retrofitting an industrial robot with 3-D printing guns and rewiring it to AI, so the machine can see its own structure while building and learn from its mistakes. The result was one of the largest models in a single piece. The Bartlett School of Architecture is now backing this work to use in more commercial projects. Another British company, AI Build, is also using AI to speed up 3-D construction.

Traditionally, when structural engineers evaluate the strength of buildings, they use approximate calculations. However, with embedded IoTs, AI could get more accurate structural stability information in real-time. The data will help AI to learn to become a better builder. As a consequence of AI's influence, 3-D printing would arguably be the most disruptive technology ever to shake the trillion-dollar global construction industry.

It is appropriate to reiterate the distinction between disruptive technologies and AI. The disruptive technologies like 3-D printing, autonomous cars, drone delivery of goods, and a zillion others are popping up all over the globe in a very short period of time. Faster computers also gave birth to AI, which is now further disrupting every other disruptive technology. Three-D printing technology is one of its victims.

Should construction workers be worried? Yes, they should be. They should attempt to learn technologies such as 3-D printer design, 3-D printer manufacturing, 3-D printer marketing, 3-D printer R&D, 3-D printer retail part selling, etc. All of those industries will enjoy cascading growth in the future.

Although AI would threaten a large number of unskilled jobs in the construction industry, the sheer volume of construction made possible by 3-D technology would absorb many of the job losses for a while at least. Then as automation consumes more businesses, unskilled workers will find it harder to hang in there. This category of unemployed workers will badly need UBI, which as we previously noted would not be practical until house prices are affordable.

Today a three-bedroom, three-bathroom house averages around $300,000. Consider how the real estate market might shift if we incorporate 3-D technology and the same house can be built for $60,000 or less. Lower-income families would breathe a sigh of relief while the rich could afford more houses. Both scenarios would mean a significant increase in housing demand, creating a significant number of jobs. Of course, most of the jobs will be high-tech jobs.

In the United States nearly 34 percent of an average worker's income goes toward housing. For the poor the percentage is even higher. The general population will embrace 3-D-constructed housing because their mortgage burden would substantially lower. If you look at it pragmatically, the positive impact of 3-D printing on the economy will outweigh its negative impact of job losses.

From the employment perspective, 3-D construction is a huge game changer. Now imagine the impact of low-cost construction on the rest of the economy. 3-D construction significantly impacts the cost of building structures like shopping malls, warehouses, office buildings, industrial buildings, and so on. Low cost means more economic activity and higher living standard. Although AI takes away most of the manual jobs, it creates a plethora of skilled jobs increasing societal abundance. With AI-induced abundance, the unemployed who are the victims of this tech disruption can afford basic lives with their share of UBI.

Just to bring costs into perspective, in August 2005 Hurricane Katrina resulted in $105 billion in damage with 1,836 total fatalities. If the cities and towns had been built using 3-D technology, the losses would have been significantly lower. As 3-D printing technology evolves, the financial loss from natural disasters will come down and have less and less impact on the overall economy. We can also quickly rebuild those lost townships and industries resulting in lower economic damage. Governments around the world should consider offering subsidies, tax write-offs and other incentives for 3-D printed houses, especially in hurricane areas, where global warming is creating ever more powerful storms. Similarly, insurance companies should encourage AI driven technologies to rebuild houses, so the financial risk is lowered.

The bottom line is, there is every reason to embrace intelligent 3-D technology. It appears to take away our jobs, while in reality it creates abundance making the global economy much stronger than what we have today.

Chapter 4

Reinvesting Transportation

Transportation is crucial to the global economy. While AI would substantially bring down the cost of transportation thereby boosting the economic growth and increasing societal abundance that could contain unemployment, it would also threaten transportation jobs.

When I booked my first Tesla Model 3, I was only two hours late, and my booking number was 150,000. No car maker in the history of automobile manufacturing had ever sold that many cars online so quickly—and before the company even had a site to assemble it. After that shock the entire auto industry woke up from hibernation and started scrambling to switch over to electric car technology just to survive the competition.

With all the car makers producing electric cars, imagine what the impact will be on the industries that are dependent on gasoline cars as more people switch to electric vehicles. A whole lot of businesses would fold. Gas stations would obviously be one of the front liners. There are more than half a million gas stations in the United States alone. Out of those only a few would survive as charging stations. The rest don't stand a chance.

The next shockwave yet to come is self-driving or autonomous technology. In this book I use the words *self-driving* and *autonomous* interchangeably, both meaning *driverless*. Interestingly, these terminologies have different meanings in other parts of the world. In India for instance, *self-driving* refers to a regular car without a hired driver, meaning you have to drive your rental car by yourself and no driver will be provided. For non-Indians that definition might seem odd, but traditionally in India, rentals used to always come with a driver. Only recently have car rental companies in the country started offering driverless—as in chauffer-less—cars. So please be aware of the regional slangs.

Although Tesla, Google, and Uber appear to be in the forefront of the game, pretty much every car manufacturer has invested heavily in this technology, and we will soon see countless numbers of self-driving electric cars on the market. Although autonomous technology could fit into any car type be it electric or gasoline, most autonomous cars on the market today are electric.

For these obvious reasons, in this book autonomous refers to self-driving electric car technology.

Here is what autonomous transport technology can offer us. It could prevent hundreds of thousands of traffic crashes, save millions of gallons of fuel, and free up time for countless numbers of commuters. Reduction in traffic accidents means saving billions of dollars in healthcare costs. Decades ago there were fewer vehicles and fewer accidents. According to the National Highway Traffic Safety Administration (NHTSA), US motor vehicle crashes per year cost over $1 trillion in loss of productivity and loss of life.

As most self-driving cars on the market today are electric, reduction in gasoline usage means better health with cleaner air. Bear in mind that a reduction in gasoline usage in cars does not mean less CO_2 emission. Electric cars need power, and we obviously would burn more coal or natural gas to produce electricity to feed the electric car market. We are just shifting the CO_2 emission problem from cars to power plants. However, when cars become electric, they have the option of using electricity produced by solar power plants. Many people have solar panels installed on their rooftops to feed electric cars. The point is, mere conversion of gasoline technology to electric technology will not help the environment; however, it opens an opportunity for solar evolution. At the same time cities are saved from gasoline pollution. Some cities in the world are almost uninhabitable because of the smog caused by gasoline burning. Environmentalists claim that breathing in Delhi, India, is equivalent to smoking forty cigarettes a day.

What's Slowing Down the Autonomous Car Industry

Self-driving technology is all set to hit the road. What slowing down its arrival are the legalities. Legal experts are still figuring out how to deal with accidents caused by this new technology. In today's world, the legal processes and procedures are pretty much in place for human drivers. As it stands, drivers are currently legally accountable for accidents in traditional cars. But with self-driven cars, there are other considerations. The car owner, the car manufacturer, and the software provider invariably get into the legal tussle. Many legal complications have to be ironed out. Until then self-driving will just be an add-on feature turned on at the driver's risk. In all Tesla vehicles, the drivers have to keep touching the steering wheel every few minutes to keep the automated system going. This is a precaution to make sure that the driver is awake while in auto-mode. That is the stage we are in now. Technology is ready but not the regulations.

Accidents in Autonomous Cars

In self-driving cars, if you look at it pragmatically, safety is all about data. Most car crashes happen because of a lack of data. We blame automation for accidents, but in reality it is the real-time data that saves lives.

Take the example of the 2016 Tesla crash that occurred in Florida. The autopilot sensors on the Model S failed to distinguish a white tractor-trailer crossing the highway against a bright sky. This is an automated system that is fully dependent on data for safety. If you want to blame someone, it's the missing data. This accident could have been easily averted in multiple ways if you examine it from a data perspective. First off, if the system had topological data coming from satellites, like real-time Google Earth, it would have figured out that there was a tractor-trailer crossing the highway. The second possibility would have been that if the tractor-trailer itself were transmitting data—the way airplane transponders do—that in turn was captured, then the crash could have been easily averted. The third possibility would be if any other automated vehicle on the road saw the tractor-trailer crossing the highway and had that data been shared, then the crash could have been successfully averted.

In the near future as more vehicles become automated, there will be more data on the roads, you can visualize it as a kind of data superhighway, every vehicle will know every other vehicle on that road, and these kinds of dumb accidents won't happen.

Safety is all about the availability of data. This means our future vehicles will be filled with the Internet of things (IoT) in all critical parts sending real-time data, so AI would process it and maneuver it safely. That means no surprise brake failures or engine outages. Every crucial component will be sending data via IoTs, and AI would know the exact safety level of the vehicle before the tires hit the road. If the vehicle is not safe enough, the vehicle won't even start.

The other exciting thing is that in the autonomous world, all vehicles on the road would be exchanging data. Even the satellites would be grabbing and throwing back immense amounts of data for safety. It would truly be a magical digital world. While such data would be invaluable as far as safety is concerned, in the same breath it's overwhelming too. This is where AI would become an invaluable asset to decipher this towering bigdata and direct the autonomous systems to work safely.

It is not hard to imagine that in the digital future AI would easily figure out not just a tractor-trailer passing in front, but in fact it could even predict the position of all the vehicles for miles ahead via the flood of real-time data. For automated vehicles *data is the eye, data is the brain; if data is missing it is blind.* This explains the Tesla crash scenario. In the future we expect that as data grows exponentially, safety concerns will fade out.

The Darkside of Self-Driving

In self-driving cars the sensors need to be in flawless condition all the time. If a mechanic makes a mistake, it could cost human lives. The mechanics of the future will be under greater stress, and the job demands a higher technical skill level.

This will take us to a new world of sensor-anxiety. In today's manually-driven cars even if the engine breaks down, at least you have control of the vehicle. But in driverless cars, you are at the mercy of those sensors. Sensor anxiety might be so worrisome that it raises the question: is car ownership really worth it. Then how about just summoning a self-driving cab when you need one? With an autonomous taxi, you not only stop worrying about the sensor, but you also don't have to deal with any car maintenance period. For car rental companies, it's economically feasible to maintain a large fleet of cabs, develop sophisticated AI logs and monitor them constantly to make sure all vehicles are in good shape. They could supplement sensor data with a multitude of exchangeable data on the digital superhighway so that vehicles don't have to depend only on sensors—what a relief.

At some point in the future, human drivers will become a rarity, and gasoline cars will be relegated to vintage clubs. With all gasoline cars outdated, gas stations shutting down, and car ownership a rarity, the automobile industry will move into the next era of digital transport fully managed by artificial intelligence (AI).

Here is how the future of commute could look like. On a typical day, you get up in the morning, get ready to go to work and summon a cab or the AI in your smart home could summon your favorite car. When you board the car, the AI in the car uses its facial recognition technology to know who you are, where your office is, and even what credit card to charge. All you need to say is: *Go to the office,* and it will take you to your office in the shortest possible time depending on the traffic situation on that day. You can totally focus on tasks of value during transport without being distracted and have the same comfy ride coming back home. As there is no human driver in the cab, the cost of the ride will be a fraction of what it normally costs with a driver.

Suppose if your office is far away and the journey is too long or not suitable for car commute, the cab will take you to the nearest train/bus station. The AI in your phone App would direct you to the intended train/bus. You board the train/bus, and when the destination is reached, you come out of the train/bus, and another cab will be waiting to pick you up. Here again, the cab knows who you are and where your office is. You don't have to be anxious about the route it takes or the number of trains/buses it suggests or anything of that sort. You just follow the directions from the AI, and it will take you to your destination in the shortest possible time depending on the traffic situation on that day. You can totally focus on tasks of value during transport without being distracted. Same comfy ride coming back home. What a hassle-free commute. It certainly bolsters the productivity at workplaces.

In this example the entire commute is dependent upon data: the data of routes, data on traffic conditions, data of train/buses schedules, personal data of passenger, and so on. AI will put all this together and save you plenty of time. Once we get into these kinds of AI scripted grand comforts, there will be no turning back.

There could still be a few people who wish to own and drive cars for fun. People could even continue to drive gasoline cars, as long as gasoline continues to be sold. Insurance companies will charge them exuberant premiums as they are risky human ventures amid safe digital transportation. When all gas stations are completely rolled down, it will ultimately make the ownership of gasoline cars obsolete.

Birth of Creepy Cabs

The idea of digital transport is indeed creepy. Every cab on the street knows who is sitting in them, and the cars would exchange information so swiftly that the entire fleet of cars in a city could be easily tracked. It might feel like an invasion of privacy, but that is what we chose. Loss of privacy is not happening by accident; we let it happen intentionally in the name of comfort and luxury. And we love the luxury AI offers. There is no turning back.

Talking about privacy, regular folks who commute to work every day need not be uptight. In fact, that would give them a legit alibi to prove they have a normal life. Anything strange should certainly be accounted for. This helps keep the communities safe.

The Job Threat

Cab drivers would obviously be one of the front liners. It is estimated that in the United States alone more than four million taxi and truck drivers would lose their jobs when manual driving is fully taken over by autonomous technology.

As the world makes its transition from car ownership to car usership, we could see many companies flaunting their fleet of autonomous cars for the public to rent and roll. It could be rental car companies like Hertz and Alamo, taxi companies like Uber and Ola, or direct car manufacturers like GM and Ford that get into this lucrative car rental business.

When so many companies begin to compete on the road, consumer expectation will change profusely. They expect the autonomous car to be stylish, clean, and luxurious with all the latest features; otherwise, they will just dismiss it and summon another. Clunkers don't stand a chance. That will tremendously impact the volume of car manufacturing. In order to maintain new cars on the road, the competing companies will have to recycle cars frequently. In today's world, we keep our cars on average between ten and fifteen years. In the automated future, you may not see cars that are older than a few months, which means the number of cars manufactured could increase by almost a thousand-fold. Consequently, car manufacturing facilities will begin to pop up like mushrooms all over the country, leading to massive employment and entrepreneurial opportunities. However, most of these will be assembled by robots, likely meaning that the employment opportunities will cater to the technologically skilled although some unskilled workers could be rehired for a while until automation fully takes over.

The other major job creator in the car industry indeed would be car detailing. With customer expectations hitting the roof, it would be expedient for the cars to be impeccably detailed after each use. This competitive market opens up a host of new opportunities in car detailing, servicing, and monitoring. This will flare up many jobs, careers, and entrepreneurial opportunities—but again, all whirling around high technology. The car detailers of the future will not be cleaning cars with hands but with robots. Humans will be remotely monitoring thousands of such stations. Yes, jobs are plentiful but highly skilled.

With most driving jobs gone, the cost of transportation would be rock bottom. The cost of transportation is now dependent on the cost of automation and the cost of energy. I have dedicated a separate chapter to discuss how AI could cut the cost of energy further enhancing the societal abundance.

Along Comes the Hyperloop

Autonomous driving is only a part of the story of transportation evolution. The long-distance commute and cargo transportation are still sluggish despite autonomous technology. At the very opportune time, just when the world is craving for high-speed transportation, there emerges a new technology called *'Hyperloop'* that has the capability to disrupt the transportation sector even more severely than autonomous technology.

Today our global transportation is moving at snail speed. Ships take almost a month to cross oceans. Even the fastest international passenger airlines can take more than a day to fly half-way across the globe. We are paying a huge price in terms of slow economic growth for this sluggish travel. For elderly people global travel is a nightmare.

Global transport is slow because of fuel efficiency. Shipping companies save fuel costs by traveling at an optimal speed of 20 knots (23 mph). Anything more and ship safety will be compromised, and at the same time more fuel will be used. A speed of 20 knots is ridiculous; however, on the sea it's the best we get.

The same reasoning goes with airlines too. Airlines go at speeds for optimal fuel use. Recommended cruising speeds for commercial airliners today range between about 480 and 510 knots. Going faster eats more fuel per passenger-mile. As of today, 600 mph is the limit we could reach. This speed is plentiful compared to land travel; however, for long distances it looks darn slow.

For any global economy that acutely depends on shipping, a month of ship travel from one end of the globe to the other can only be described as deplorable. All the economic parameters like the cost of inventory, delivery time, even the marketability of a product, profoundly depend on speed. Even though the cost of transportation initially seems higher using higher speeds, the reduction in inventory and high-volume delivery would balance it out. Economies would grow more rapidly with speed. Global economies, especially in the advanced world, are craving for high-speed transportation.

Now let's talk about the culprits of today's stunted transportation. When it comes to air travel, wind friction is the cause for limited speed.

At sea, water resistance is the speed breaker. For high-speed trains it's air drag. When it comes to road transport, it's the human at the wheel that puts the break on speed for safety.

When we put all this together, the two things that stand out in preventing high speed are drag and safety. The obvious approach that comes to mind is an enclosed transport where air can be sucked out, reducing the drag, and at the same time with safety IoT restraints, the AI-maneuvered vehicles can go safely at high speeds. The only limitation to the speed would then be the sophistication of the technology. Let's look at some of the global efforts in pursuit of high-speed transport.

Elon Musk (Tesla, SpaceX) first publicly announced his idea of a hyperloop in 2012 that would use reduced-pressure tubes in which passenger pods ride on air bearings. His concept of the Hyperloop Alpha was first published in August 2013. SpaceX has built an operational hyperloop test system at its headquarters in Hawthorne, California. It's approximately one mile long with a six-foot outer diameter. To encourage innovation SpaceX announced the Hyperloop Pod Competition to challenge college student teams to build the best transport pod. In the first competition, held in January 2017, below are the winners:

> Overall Score: Delft Hyperloop (Delft University of Technology, Netherlands)
>
> Fastest Pod Award: WARR Hyperloop (Technical University of Munich, Germany)
>
> Safety and Reliability: MIT Hyperloop (MIT, USA)
>
> Pod Innovation Award: Badgerloop (University of Wisconsin, USA) and rLoop (Reddit)
>
> Best Performance in Operations: UMDloop (University of Maryland, USA)

In the August 2017 competition, the first prize went to WARR Hyperloop. In the July 2018 competition, WARR Hyperloop pod hits 284 mph to win SpaceX competition.

The hyperloop concept was open-sourced by SpaceX so people across the globe could take the idea and further develop it. SpaceX also provides services to innovators and universities across the world interested in high-speed transportation technology and solutions.

Since then many companies have been formed and are working to advance the technology. The company Hyperloop One has proposed a business case for a three-hundred-mile hyperloop route between Helsinki and Stockholm that would tunnel under the Baltic Sea and take less than thirty minutes. Hyperloop One is also doing a feasibility study for hyperloop routes between Dubai and the greater United Arab Emirates. It is studying a cargo hyperloop to connect Hunchun in China to Russia's Far East.

In May 2016 Hyperloop One kicked off a global challenge for comprehensive proposals of potential hyperloop networks around the world and selected proposals for the following ten routes: Toronto/Montreal, Cheyenne/Denver/Pueblo, Miami/Orlando, Dallas/Laredo/Houston, Chicago/Columbus/Pittsburgh, Mexico City/Guadalajara, Edinburgh/London, Glasgow/Liverpool, Bengaluru/Chennai, and Mumbai/Pune.

Hyperloop One was rebranded as Virgin Hyperloop One after a substantial investment from the Virgin Group led by Richard Branson. Virgin Hyperloop One has also built a fully operational test site in Nevada.

Another company, Hyperloop Transportation Technologies (HTT) USA, is doing preliminary studies to link Bratislava, Vienna, and Budapest. It is doing similar explorations to connect Bratislava, Brno, and Prague.

It looks like India is a strong market for hyperloops as well. Many companies are competing here too. HTT has proposed a hyperloop route between Chennai and Bengaluru, taking a half-hour. HTT is also proposing to link Amaravathi to Vijayawada with a six-minute ride. Virgin Hyperloop One has proposed a route between Pune and Mumbai, beginning with an operational demonstration track. Indore-based D GWHyperloop is proposing a hyperloop between Mumbai and Delhi.

AI to Make Hyperloop Cheaper

One of the roadblocks in the evolution of hyperloop technology is the expensive infrastructure. Tunneling is one of the biggest costs. Today's hyperloop technologies are depending on huge tunneling machines worth millions of dollars. These are not only expensive to manufacture, but they are also very pricey to transport and install at the site. Even the operation of such tunnel drilling machines requires an inordinate amount of energy. If the machine breaks down for any reason, the project comes to a screeching halt until it is repaired and put back to work. The entire drilling task depends on this expensive machine. This problem is being reevaluated by many entrepreneurs by using AI. Instead of one large drilling machine, they are considering replacing it with millions of ant-like robots. Ant locomotion could be the future of robotic tunneling systems.

Research conducted by the Georgia Institute of Technology's School of Physics studied fire ants in laboratory settings. Using video and X-ray computed tomography, researchers have uncovered fundamentals of ant locomotion in digging tunnels that future robotics could use. This was sponsored by the National Science Foundation. Similar studies were done at the New Jersey Institute of Technology as well.

The robot ant tunneling technique, if it becomes a reality, could dramatically change the landscape of hyperloop. These tiny robots could burrow holes like ants do instead of one huge expensive drilling rig. Each of these bugs would carry its own batteries that could get frequently charged. We could easily mass produce millions of these little bugs and use the army of little drillers to build the tunnel economically. If programmed well, the entire army of ants could be fully controlled by AI, making it completely autonomous. If one ant fails, it will not be a show-stopper. These ant bots would also evolve as AI learns from them.

There are already commercial ventures in Europe in this direction. Badger is a consortium consisting of seven partners from five different European countries. Its goal is to design and develop a small, worm-like, autonomous underground robotic system that would drill, map, and navigate underground space. It uses a conventional rotary cutting head with an ultrasonic drill, which pulverizes rock with high-frequency sound waves. The soil will then be sent to the surface. It moves forward like a worm. The rear part of this worm will clamp itself to the wall. As it moves it will reinforce the tunnel behind it using a 3-D printer.

In the future with these less expensive, easily mass-producible, self-learning, self-evolving mini bots all steered by AI, we won't need expensive tunneling machines anymore.

Hyper-Safety with AI

Just as with any other transport, in hyperloop technology speed and safety are mutually exclusive. In this super high-speed transport, data is life and death. We need data from every corner of the transport system. This should remind us of the sensory organs of AI: the IoTs. The hyperloop needs millions of IoTs embedded in every critical system like a propulsion system, transmission system, suspension system, braking system, electrical system, and so on. We also need IoTs on the tunnel structure of the hyperloop to get data on structural stability. We need IoTs pretty much on every critical component to monitor the system for safety and stability. The more data, the better.

What do you think would handle this immense amount of big data sucked in from all IoTs? AI's capability to make decisions becomes indispensable. AI can look at the mounds of data and prognosticate if anything would compromise safety. As AI gets real-time data, there are no surprise part failures. All the future failures would have been predicted and taken care of well before the journey starts. Any unexpected outside forces like earthquakes or bomb explosions are sensed in real-time and would bring the system to a halt.

AI can even suggest alternative ways to improve hyperloop technology to augment both speed and safety. For example, it may do analytics on big data and suggest alternate aerodynamic shapes of the pods traveling inside the loop or economical propulsion system to increase fuel efficiency or alternate suspension system to increase safety and so on. In the future, if all the hyperloop systems around the world talk to each other, AI would learn and continuously evolve offering us better safety. Think of AI as an efficient designer, builder, and operator. Hyperloop can't ignore AI in its evolution.

Now imagine the impact of this cheap transport on the economy. Both autonomous driving and hyperloop transport affects the cost of everything we buy. With AI-induced abundance, the unemployed can easily afford basic lives with their share of UBI.

Looks like we are becoming more comfortable now talking about UBI as housing and transportation would become affordable in the new era of AI.

Chapter 5

Inventively Serving Food

This chapter we will explore how AI would threaten our jobs in the food industry and at the same time substantially reducing the cost of food thereby increasing societal abundance. As food is the basic need for human survival and also part of a strong global economy, any technology that cuts its cost down would flareup the economy and at the same time counter the hunger of the victims of this technological disruption.

Wouldn't it be enthralling to order food in our own kitchens just like we do in restaurants, with chef-quality food arriving promptly at our table? That's where the food industry is heading now. UK-based Moley Robotics has developed The Moley Robotic Kitchen, which the company says "is revolutionary for more than its automated cooking; it is also an iTunes-style library with a growing collection of recipes from around the world. Initially it starts with a plate of ingredients. Eventually the system will be accessed anywhere remotely, with a delicious meal awaiting your arrival home."

After placing separate containers of measured, washed, and cut ingredients on designated spots and pressing the start button, the Moley will download the recipe from the Internet and cook. It will even clean up after itself.

The food industry is a highly labor-intensive sector, and the price is largely related to manual labor costs. Harvesting, transportation, warehousing, and even food preparation are the services that add cost to food. AI is establishing itself in all these areas, which could have a phenomenal effect in terms of reducing the cost. I have been following some of the disruptions that are happening in the food industry and below are a few of them.

The company Harvest Robotics has developed a strawberry picking machine that can serve eight acres in one day, doing work equivalent to thirty workers. Harvesting machines are not new to the agriculture industry. However, the latest AI-driven machines use object recognition software to identify multiple types of fruits. They are very efficient as they self-learn and learn from other machines. As there are worker shortages in many parts of California and

Florida, these machines are keeping the industry going.

Blue River Technology, owned by John Deere, has developed a robotic weed killer that can identify the weeds using AI and spray herbicides with high precision, reducing the cost of weed control. The AI needs a large amount of varied data including varieties of weeds so that the machine can learn to differentiate between a plant and a weed. This kind of AI-assisted weed control can save almost $40 billion annually on just weed control itself, a huge game changer in agriculture.

Although chemical weed killers seem revolutionary, they have their own chemical footprint. They also give rise to herbicide-resistant superweeds which are part of today's reality. Chemicals are highly harmful to our ecosystem, although they seem to do wonders in the short term. Fortunately many alternative technologies are on the way. The US Department of Agriculture is experimenting with sandblasting weeds. Norwegian University is experimenting on killing weeds with lasers. All these technologies would greatly challenge the agrochemical companies that are dominating today's market.

Many research studies are underway to develop crawling, climbing, buzzing micro-robots or weedbots that can bite-off the weeds instead of killing them with chemicals. These weedbots maneuvered by AI, will be highly economical and eco-friendly. According to current research outcomes, few weedbots could easily manage an acre of a plantation. They can also be programmed to protect the plants from pests, insects and other crop destroyers again avoiding pesticides. They can even look after the health of the plants by sampling their tissue-data and advice the plantation owners about the maintenance needed to increase the yield. Possibilities are endless if AI is harnessed well.

SkySquirrel has developed an AI technology that uses drones to take aerial pictures of vineyards. It compares the photos of grape leaves to its database to detect diseases, pests, and poor plants. This saves tons of money in manual labor required for maintenance.

Sorting fruits and vegetables is yet another labor-intensive task that employs about two million people. Tomra Systems uses AI in its fruit and vegetable sorters, which uses technologies like infra-red spectroscopy. The Japanese company Kewpie is using Google's TensorFlow machine learning software to quickly inspect ingredients that go into food products. With AI, these companies can achieve good results at substantially reduced costs.

AI is also being developed to capture popular recipes. Coca-Cola has devised a unique way to learn user preferences. It has installed self-service soft drink fountains in numerous restaurants, where customers can mix and match and create their own flavored drinks. This data was fed to AI to figure out what the majority of customers want and came up with a new flavor. AI recommended Cherry Sprite to be a favored combination, and Coke eventually launched the product. In the coming years we will see more of such AI generated recipes in the food industry.

Researchers at the University of Nottingham in the UK in conjunction with the company Martec of Whitwell have come up with an AI technology that uses ultrasonic sensing and optical fluorescence imaging technologies to monitor how food processing equipment is cleaned. This reduces water use, energy, and time, saving millions of dollars.

Looking at all these developments, AI is pretty much everywhere from seeding to harvesting to cooking food. AI is going to disrupt the food industry massively both in terms of jobs and reducing the cost of food.

Impending Job Losses

In the food industry most of the jobs are done by unskilled manual laborers, so job losses will be rampant as AI takes over. But one unique thing with the food industry is that the number of restaurants, the number of grocery shops, the number of food trucks, are all limited by population size. Meaning the food industry can't grow endlessly because we eat a limited quantity of food every day. We may eat varieties, but the quantity is limited. Obviously this industry may not absorb all the unskilled workers who lose their jobs as a consequence of AI. At the same time it creates an umpteen number of skilled jobs and huge entrepreneurial opportunities for startups.

From seeding to cooking, if all acts are done by machines, imagine the quality of food. Food is grown, harvested, transported, warehoused, and finally delivered by the machines. Even in a house the food is cooked by a machine. If all these machines are under the tight supervision of AI, then we can easily draw a relation between our health and what is grown out there. This becomes a single, super-grid of the food world.

Global researches are already underway to grow food in vertical buildings under artificial light reducing the land usage, water consumption, pesticide menace and substantially insulating the crops from flood and drought. This decentralized food production would reduce the need for transportation. Instead of growing crops in specific areas and then transporting it across the globe, it would make economic sense to grow and serve in local areas. The only challenge is artificially creating those varied climatic conditions that mimic mother nature. And when these ventures are commercialized they will have a dramatic effect on international shipping and import/export of commodities.

There isn't a sane reason for anyone to paint AI as a job killer in the food industry. Although AI takes away most of the manual jobs, it creates many skilled jobs and new business opportunities. Low-cost, high-quality food means higher living standards and societal abundance. Cheap food means lighter saddle on the governments that support subsidized food for the poor and unemployed. The food stamps that cost the government billions of dollars will suddenly become less burdensome. If governments are serious about supporting the unemployed, AI shouldn't be ignored in the food industry.

Chapter 6

Intelligent Care of Health

This chapter discusses two burning topics in healthcare: AI's ability to deflate skyrocketing healthcare costs and the impending job losses in healthcare stemming from AI takeover.

Amid dissensions, economic pundits agree on one thing: technology is driving our rising healthcare costs. Isn't it a bit outlandish? The same technology that made the laptops, mobile phones, and other gadgets smarter, made them cheaper too. Why on earth would technology make healthcare expensive?

The difference is consumer electronics are products, while healthcare is a service. Laptops and mobile phones are mass-produced and exported worldwide, bringing down their cost. Global competition has made these products low-cost. Sadly, healthcare is a highly doctor subservient and hospital-reliant service that is hard to globalize—for now.

Just to illustrate this dependency, say a patient goes to a hospital with a kidney stone. With the current technology, the stone can be fragmented and removed in a simple outpatient procedure. However, to get to that point is a long journey. In most cases patients arrive at an emergency room with severe abdominal pain. They get checked up by physicians, who order some lab tests or scans, and then the patient is moved to the procedure room. When all is said and done, the patient has utilized expensive resources including physicians, nurses, technicians, etc. This is how the cost escalates even if the actual treatment is simple. This kind of doctor reliance is not there in electronic gadgets.

If the laptop or mobile phone manufacturers invest billions of dollars in bringing out the next great feature, the cost is easily absorbed when millions of customers worldwide purchase the device. That is not the case with healthcare, where if there is a new invention, it can't be sold directly to the patients. It has to be approved by the Federal Drug Administration, adopted by the hospitals, protocols have to be set, and all the healthcare professionals have to be trained to use it. There is a huge service dependency that makes it cost sensitive.

How Expensive Is Healthcare Anyway?

According to the United States Department of Health and Human Services, the total healthcare spending in 1970 was about $75 billion, or only $356 per person. In less than 50 years, these costs have grown to $2.2 trillion, or $7,421 per person.

Advanced medical technologies continue to increase longevity and improve the quality of life for many Americans. However, sophisticated medical technologies result in expensive treatments and is a major cause of higher healthcare costs today.

It is estimated that healthcare costs for chronic disease treatments account for more than 75 percent of national healthcare expenditures. Advanced medical technologies diagnose more and more people with new problems every day, increasing the number of patients receiving treatment.

As recently as a few decades ago, diagnosing cancer was relatively rare. Now, doctors diagnose many types of cancers on a regular basis. We simply did not have the tools or technology to diagnose it as easily in the past. Once diagnosed these diseases have to be treated.

The cost of healthcare could be attenuated by maneuvering these expensive technologies with AI making them more efficient and less doctor subservient.

This chapter is fully devoted to such deliberations.

The AI Leverage

Here is an example of maneuvering expensive healthcare technologies with AI. The average cost of a colonoscopy in the United States is over $3,000 and takes about upwards of an hour for the procedure. Believe it or not, the success rate of detecting benign polyps is not 100 percent. It means that a doctor could possibly miss cancerous polyps during a colonoscopy, resulting in expensive procedures later on, adding to the healthcare cost. Remember; every undetected polyp escalates the cost of healthcare.

This is where AI has a significant role to play. Using its object recognition capability, AI can identify patterns and is capable of comparing the scanned image against the millions of data inputs from patients around the world. Doctors at Showa University in Yokohama, Japan, were able to scan for polyps with high accuracy. AI-assisted colonoscopy technologies are much more efficient and reliable compared to those done by humans alone.

AI systems can also look at more than three hundred features of polyps in less than a second. In an AI-assisted colonoscopy, if a doctor misses a polyp, AI would see it and send an alert so the doctor could go back and take a second look in the same procedure. This dramatically increases the efficiency of scanning and substantially reduces overall healthcare costs by preventing patient readmissions—not to mention the suffering that follows wrong diagnoses.

Scientists at Stanford University created an AI diagnosis algorithm for skin cancer using a Google-provided public application programming interface—a set of routines, protocols, and tools for building software and applications. They made a database of nearly 130,000 skin disease images and trained their algorithm to diagnose potential cancer visually. The algorithm was tested against twenty-one board-certified dermatologists. In its diagnoses of skin lesions, which represented the most common and deadliest skin cancers, the algorithm matched the performance of dermatologists, with a whopping 91 percent accuracy rate. Here again higher efficiency, less doctor time, and fewer wrong diagnoses would reduce healthcare costs considerably.

Robots in Surgery

Have you seen a da Vinci surgical robot in action on YouTube? It's amazing to watch how a robot can operate on a human being. Though human surgeons are still needed, the surgical procedure itself is robot-intensive. Surgeons have moved away from the operating table to nearby control stations where they control the operating robots the way players control video games. The surgeons use their surgical knowledge, which is complemented by the precision cutting and stitching done by the machine.

There are many companies competing in the field of robotic surgery, but Intuitive's da Vinci was the first to become well-established in the market.

Robotic surgery provides patients with less discomfort and has quicker recovery time, so the technology reduces hospital costs by shortening hospital stays; there are also fewer readmissions after the procedures, which lead to reduced overall healthcare cost. As of now robot-surgery is used for colorectal, gynecological, head, neck, thoracic, and urological procedures. Every year robotics performs about 2 million surgical procedures globally, with over half of them done in the United States alone.

The AI Intervention in Robotic Surgery

Although robotic surgery appears to be highly advanced, AI influence is still very minimal. It is still a human-controlled procedure. Many surgeons today are being trained to use this technology and at academic level medical students go through residency and fellowship programs that focus on robotic surgery.

Surgery robots are just hard-coded robots that function as programmed. They lack a brain. The brain is still the human surgeon. But AI by definition has the potential to intercede.

A Johns Hopkins University research team developed a robotic surgical system called the smart tissue-autonomous robot (STAR) that can integrate 3-D imaging and sensors to help guide the robot through the suturing process.

Google has teamed up with Johnson and Johnson to develop a robotic surgical device that uses AI to learn human anatomy. This is a surgical game changer. It may not help a well-versed surgeon but greatly helps new doctors during their training. And as these young, robotic surgeons progress into the future, they will depend more heavily on the technologies they have been trained with.

AI is slowly replacing hardcoded robotic technology into more flexible self-learning, adaptable systems.

Although this looks like a threat to the surgical profession, it's a great opportunity for new professions to emerge to support the new technology. Highly-skilled professionals will be needed to build, improve, and manage AI surgical systems. A new field called medical engineering is already evolving, which requires knowledge of both medicine and engineering. In the future, even though we may not see surgeons at the operating table, highly skilled medical engineers will be working behind the scenes developing and improving AI-surgical robots.

Using AI to Detect Tuberculosis

Researchers at Thomas Jefferson University Hospital in Philadelphia are training AI to detect tuberculosis (TB). AI is learning from a host of medical images to interpret radiographs for the presence of TB. These kinds of fully automated technologies will substantially bring down the cost of healthcare.

Using AI to Detect Brain Bleeds

IBM Watson and Israel-based MedyMatch Technology are coming together to use AI to help doctors detect brain bleeds resulting from head trauma and stroke. It uses machine learning algorithms that have access to machine vision and patient data to highlight areas of potential presence of cerebral bleeds. Any kind of automation that enhances efficiency substantially reduces healthcare costs.

I hope these examples give you a glimpse of the healthcare industry that is now being heavily intervened by AI. The reality is AI needs enormous amounts of data for effectiveness, be it diagnostics or procedural. It means that the more data we collect from the human body, the better it is for AI to bring down the cost of healthcare. Let's discuss how AI could enter the field of data collection from the human body.

Diagnostics with Big Data

Healthcare and human body big data are tightly coupled; in reality they are one and the same.

When you go to a doctor with symptoms of an ailment, diagnosis begins with some questions. Then the doctor could check you physically and may also order lab tests. Once those results arrive, the doctor will analyze them using the medical knowledge to arrive at the best diagnosis.

If you look at this routine process in a pragmatic way, a medical diagnosis is nothing but analytics of human body big data. Here the word *data* collectively means patient symptoms, patient lab results, patient's medical history, the doctor's medical knowledge and past experiences in treating similar ailments, etc. If the doctor has not treated an ailment before then, their academic knowledge is the only valuable resource.

Every time there is a new medical breakthrough, the doctors will learn about it from medical journals or attending conferences. Every time a new ailment is treated, the doctor's knowledge enhances. Every time the doctor misdiagnoses, they will learn from the mistakes. There is a constant learning process in medicine that leads to more reliable diagnoses over time. It's this learning process that AI is now challenging.

Today medical knowledge is digitally available online and in journals, books, and publications. Doctors' experiences are now being digitally recorded in all hospitals in the form of electronic medical records (EMR), a huge amount of data varied both in ethnicity and demography. Every time there is a research breakthrough, medical knowledge will be immediately available in digital publications. Every time a new ailment is treated, it shows up on a patient's EMR. There is a constant update of digital information in real time.

Before the digital revolution, a doctor's experiences stayed in their memory, with only a fraction making it to journals and books. Now that information is instantly available in digital format. The human element that stored that information is slowly becoming obsolete. This is a significant development in medicine.

With this kind of digital information, AI is slowly moving into the field of telemedicine. Now it is possible for doctors to diagnose patients remotely. AI is capable of hashing both patient data and medical knowledge together for analytics and remote medical diagnosis. There is an umpteen number of private medical businesses already offering telemedicine bringing efficiency and swiftness into healthcare increasing patient comfort. In remote areas where there is no doctor availabile, this kind of service a life saver. During emergencies these are of immense value. Many ambulances are now being fitted with telemedicine devices where the doctors can begin diagnosis while the patient is being transported to the hospital. These kinds of services are making a big impact, particularly in highly crowded public congregations. Although telemedicine is not a full-fledged service yet and not a current threat for the medical profession, this digital diagnosis is growing very fast.

Further, if there is an outbreak of a disease or a medical research breakthrough, AI would know as soon as it became digitally available. Humans can't just compete here.

At some point in the future, it becomes inevitable for doctors to use AI in medical diagnosis and procedures to make them more efficient and cost-effective. The *next big thing* in healthcare undoubtedly is the evolution of devices that capture human body big data in real time. There is already a name for it: digital therapeutics.

Digital Therapeutics

In November 2017 the FDA approved Abilify MyCite (aripiprazole tablets with sensors). The sensor in the pill sends a message to a wearable patch when the medication is taken. The patch then transmits the information to a mobile app so that patients and doctors can track the ingestion of the medication. This is especially great for patients with dementia or mental illness, and surely this will evolve for regular patients who can't keep track of medication because of busy work schedules. Better patient management improves their health, resulting in reduced healthcare costs.

Another great digital therapeutic contribution is in the field of diabetes. For certain people with diabetes, the biggest innovation may be Dexcom's sensor, which displays glucose data on the mobile phone. A Dexcom sensor with a hair-thin wire is placed just under the skin. A transmitter clips to it and sends glucose data via Bluetooth to the Dexcom receiver and then to an iPhone. We could expect more investment to go into the monitoring of blood sugar, which will advance the technology behind preventive healthcare.

The other devices that are becoming popular are asthma inhalers. The Australian company Adherium has come up with a monitoring device for AstraZeneca's Symbicort aerosol inhaler, dubbed the SmartTouch that connects to the cloud to provide personalized feedback to patients.

Smart health tracking wearables like Fitbit are popular across the world.

All these digital therapeutic devices are innately IoTs feeding data to AI-driven apps in phones that helps patients track their own health, empowering doctors with useful data to treat patients more efficiently, reducing hospital readmissions and eventually reducing costs.

Along Comes IoTs and RFIDs in Hospitals

Have you heard of doctors operating on the wrong patients or the wrong part of the body? In busy hospitals, human errors are bound to happen. These mistakes not only escalate the cost of healthcare but cause painful suffering and even death. Many hospitals are adopting RFID tags in bracelets to identify patients and get all the patient information.

Nowadays barcodes, RFID tags, and IoT sensors are being tagged to patients, medicines and other medical instruments linking them to the Internet—empowering the field of medicine. This network has been given a new name -Wireless body area networks (WBAN). These devices monitor vital physiological data such as body temperature, blood pressure, and heart rate in real time.

Here is a glimpse into the world of digital therapy. On a typical day, a nurse while giving medication to a patient can use a mobile device to scan the patient's ID bracelet to confirm the patient's name and date of birth and to bring up their medical record and instructions for administering drugs, underpinning the five "rights" of medicine administration— the right patient, the right drug, the right dose, the right route, and the right time. The barcode on the drug packet helps to cross-check that the patient has no allergy to it. The sensors can confirm that the medication has been taken, updating the patient's EMR.

In hospitals, tracking a patient's movement inside a healthcare facility and notifying where and when the patient is required to be can save a lot of time and money. Here is a good example. The goal for angioplasty might be to have the patient operated on within sixty minutes. By tracking the patient with an IoT tag, if their progress slows, alarms can be automatically raised with senior clinicians who can intervene.

The future demand for these digital therapeutic devices will be enormous. With healthcare cost shooting up, we will see more of these devices in the market soon to improve efficiency and cut costs.

Junk Food is Cheap but Not Consequences

Junk food has literally changed the food habits of an entire generation of humans, resulting in obesity, diabetes, and other long-term health issues at very young ages around the world. Even for people who eat healthy food, it's not always possible to keep track of the calorie, especially when eating out. We are all just eating blind. The effects of blind-eating are slow to manifest, and many people only notice a health condition like obesity or diabetes or heart disease after years or even decades.

The reason for eating blindly is the lack of digital therapeutics that help us chose healthy food—for now. With a host of new devices that are flooding the market to capture the digital data coming out of the human body, we will soon be able to make better choices about what we eat. This brings the food and healthcare industry much closer, and they influence each other. It wouldn't be a surprise in the near future to see a customized menu appearing on our mobile phones as soon as we enter a restaurant. The built-in AI systems will decide what is best for us. They may even take us one step further; the restaurant's robots may use that data to prepare a customized entrée just for us. It all means one thing: in the future restaurants will prepare food keeping their customers' health in mind.

The Dark Side of AI

Amidst all the exciting news, there is a dark side to these disruptive technologies. They are forcing doctors to learn new skills. Those who can't or won't adopt the new technology might see their career stall. Nursing and other supporting personnel including hospital administration jobs are experiencing similar challenges.

Futurists are predicting massive physician unemployment at the hands of technology while the American Association of Medical Colleges predicts a physician shortfall of about 95,000 over the next decade. These predictions seem contradictory because employment shortages and unemployment scenarios are normally mutually exclusive. However, in healthcare they can coexist. Physician shortages occur because of the impact of technology. Physicians and surgeons who cannot adapt to technology—usually those who are older—will be the ones who may retire prematurely, thus causing both physician shortage and unemployment at the same time. It is not hard to visualize that very soon we will see hospitals with more young doctors who can cope with modern devices, robots, and AI.

Physician shortages may seem to increase the cost of healthcare. However, if you look at it pragmatically, every one of the healthcare technologies discussed above, when swathed in AI, requires less doctor engagement and they will have a modest price tag.

To go from a highly doctor-regimented system to doctor-less system is a unique journey in the sense that no matter how sophisticated the technology is, it's not easy to fully hand over procedures to a machine, even with the support of AI. We are ethically and legally obligated to make sure the technology is 100 percent safe. No matter how smart the da Vinci robotic surgery is, it will take a while before it becomes fully doctor-less because lives are obviously at stake. Healthcare is highly risk-centric, so the evolution of technology in healthcare will be much slower than other non-healthcare technologies. Nonetheless, that transition has begun.

The conquest of AI in healthcare will happen procedure by procedure because each one is unique. When AI completely replaces the doctor for a specific procedure, that would then have the potential to become a global product available at affordable prices. Every healthcare procedure eventually will go thru this tipping point.

Strangely enough, we don't know how AI learns. Each AI is unique in its functionality. It is hard to predict at what stage we will begin to trust AI fully in healthcare. But looking at the current developments and wide acceptance of AI, those days are not far off. Healthcare cost contraction depends on how widely AI would spread in all specialties.

AI is not a healthcare technology; it is just software that is immensely capable of processing large loads of big data to make healthcare more efficient. In the future, new healthcare procedures will inevitably come to market with built-in AI capability to fight market competition.

The doctors should pay close attention to these new AI techniques that will eventually challenge them. Physicians and surgeons of the future have to learn to live with AI by constantly upgrading their skills. Anyone who has difficulty handling high-tech will be left out. It would be wiser for healthcare professionals to learn advanced technologies early in their careers whenever the opportunity arises.

Irrefutably when routine cases and recurring chronic diseases are managed by AI, rare diseases would get the full attention of the research community, taking healthcare to the next level. Traditionally doctors and hospitals have been focusing on recurring illnesses for the revenue. However, in the future when uniqueness becomes the revenue stream, then healthcare will take a new turn. This is a tremendous, exciting entrepreneurial opportunity for doctors, who could work with research companies to market their unique clinical data from rare ailments. Doctors could also join hands with software companies to build competing AI software.

There is another upcoming technology that could significantly affect healthcare in many ways. Nanotechnology in medicine is a highly promising technology where nanobots would float in the bloodstream capturing and delivering real-time data. They are also capable of performing repairs at the cellular level and deliver drugs to specific types of cells, such as cancer cells. Any further advances in these techniques could revolutionize the way we detect and treat diseases. The global revenue from nano-enabled products is steadily growing, from $340 billion in 2010 to $730 billion in 2012 and is expected to reach $4 trillion by the end of 2019.

Imagine how efficient it would be during a robotic operation to have nanobots floating in the bloodstream sending vital data about the body. Future surgery could be a combination of robotic surgery from the outside and nano-surgery from inside.

If you look at where healthcare is heading, it all points to one direction–towards the science of data capture from the human body and its analytics. Online diagnosis, robotic surgery, preventive medicine, nanotechnology, and many other upcoming advances are all craving data for their evolution.

The takeaway is, with the arrival of AI, doctors' involvement in routine healthcare is expected to diminish. Now imagine the impact of low-cost healthcare on society. Even the poorest of the poor can afford high-quality healthcare with their share of UBI.

Before Wrapping Up

In this book I have done my best to introduce you to AI and illustrate with real-world examples the possible ways to shelter those who are or will be adversely impacted by it. However, there is one pivotal factor that I have not discussed so far and that is the impact of AI on power generation. This would dramatically cut down the cost every product on the planet, increasing global abundance to an unprecedented level.

It is appropriate to dedicate a separate chapter for this insurgence of AI. The next chapter is all about the global power surge.

Chapter 7

The Power Surge

Power surges are bound to happen when the economy rapidly expands. AI induced technologies like 3-D printing, autonomous driving, hyperloop transport, robotic food care, and so on would flare up the global economy. If the power production does not meet this demand, then the economy will suffer energy inflicted recession that we have experienced multiple times in the past decades. For this reason power generation has to be on par with, if not ahead of, the demand.

Traditional power plants do not meet the demand quickly enough, which explains energy inflicted recessions we've had. Thermal power plants and oil refineries take years or decades to complete. However, solar and wind power plants are easier to build, and they respond fairly quickly for power demand. For instance, you can get a solar roof installed and have the house generating electricity within a week. On the other hand, power grids are hard to install or expand if there is a new township. Imagine hundreds of townships that could potentially spring up in the future as a result of 3-D printing technology.

This means that as the global economy expands, we will see immense pressure on solar and wind power plants as they are cheaper to build than those that use fossil fuels. It doesn't mean that soon fossil fuel power will be replaced by solar and wind. If you look at the future power scenario in a pragmatic way, the power surge will be so high in the future that all kinds of power sources will be in demand. Solar and wind will not be competing with fossil fuels; instead, they will complement it to meet the power surge. This is where we need AI to help scale up solar and wind power generation, not only to meet the power surge but to diminish the use of fossil fuels.

Now let's look at the current power scenario and evaluate our capability to meet the future power surge.

The total global installed capacity of power (coal) is currently about 4000 GW. On top of that, every year the energy demand is increasing by almost 120 GW. But over the past ten years, our solar industry globally has grown on average only about 50 GW per year although for last two years it is a little higher, which means solar has barely satisfied the additional growth of energy demand, which again means that the world is still building more fossil fuel power plants. The process of replacing coal with solar has not even started which is a basic requirement to kill global warming, although it is a different topic for discussion. We are not going to discuss global warming in this chapter; however, I believe it is worth stressing the importance of green energies as the climate change is threatening the global economies as we build it.

Here is a quick glimpse at the current major solar power plants around the world.

2.2 GW Bhadla, India

2.0 GW Pavagada, India

1.5 GW Tengger, China

1.0 GW Datong, China

0.8 GW Longyangxia Dam, China

0.9 GW Kurnool Ultra, India

0.6 GW Kamuthi project, India

0.6 GW Rancho Cielo, USA

0.5 GW Topaz, USA

0.3 GW Noor Complex, Morocco

And there are many other smaller projects being built around the world totaling globally about 500 GW. Remember we took almost a decade to build this. Although solar is quicker to build, it is still not scalable at a global level as the market is still in its infancy stage. Not many companies are in this game, and not much investment is in place compared to the mega-fossil fuel industry on which the entire global economy is depending on. Compare this tiny 500 GW solar industry to the mighty 4000 GW of coal installations.

The world is celebrating the arrival of electric cars with the grand hope that our solar power production will step up to the demand. Sadly our solar industry is not there yet. Most electric cars are being charged at home using the traditional electric supply, which primarily comes from coal, oil, and natural gas. That means we have merely shifted the problem from cars to fossil fuel power plants. Instead of burning gasoline in the car, we are now burning the same in power plants.

Imagine the load on the power grid if all one billion vehicles with combustible engines in the world switched over to electric cars; it's estimated the additional electricity surge would reach at least 2000 GW. A total of whopping 6000 GW (4000 GW from coal + 2000 GW from vehicles) would be needed to meet this power frenzy. Considering the upcoming AI induced rapid economic growth in the very near future this demand will be many times higher.

Obviously we will start digging for more coal and oil and natural gas to meet the demand unless solar power generation grows very rapidly. As noted earlier, the fossil fuel projects take decades to complete, and our only hope is for solar not just to meet the power surge but to also establish green technology. Solar power generation is steady, reliable, and easily quantifiable from an investment point of view. Nonetheless, wind is equally competitive and is growing as a powerful complementary source to solar especially in colder seasons and regions where sunlight is not so powerful.

The Solar Success Story

Amid all the challenges, solar energy is finally becoming very competitive with fossil fuel as the price of photovoltaic modules has dropped by almost 40 percent in recent years, and the efficiency of solar cells is steadily increasing. Solar panels now account for only about a third of the cost of a power plant. To cut costs further and finally win the race with fossil fuels, an obvious solution was to put solar-robots, or solbots, to work.

California-based Alison Energy is using robots to install solar farms and substantially reducing labor costs by as much as 75 percent, making it competitive in a fossil fuel world. To reduce costs the company is using extruded concrete instead of steel to build rails. It uses robots to ride the concrete rail and clean the dust on solar modules. Also in California, SunPower is using drones to survey potential sites for a solar power farm that can fit the most solar panels to lower costs.

NEXTracker designs and builds advanced single-axis solar trackers that can intelligently track the sun and produce more power—even during cloudy days—compared to other standard tracking systems, a great boost to the solar industry.

Unquestionably, technologically advanced machines have made a towering impact on the solar industry by saving tons of money. If we can boost electricity production by 5 or 10 percent at a solar plant, that's a game changer in terms of economics. With solar intensely competing with fossil fuels, every second of solar exposure counts, and any attempt to improve solar cell efficiency has a big role to play in that industry.

AI in Solar Power Production

The science of mass-production teaches us that it is possible to produce enormous amounts of solar energy in the quickest possible time with a technique called replication. Replication is the process of producing multiple replicas of solar power plants at the same time. AI-driven robots and drones can easily bring about replication, which is exactly what we need in the energy industry today.

It's possible to program AI to manage robots and drones in assembling solar panels, transporting the panels to a power plant site, assembling a solar power plant, and then to hook up the plant to the smart grid. We are pushing AI's capability toward a fully autonomous solar-plant building system, which can sustain itself and be replicated around the world.

Once programmed these robots will perform tirelessly until the power plant assembly is complete. Initially the cost will be high, as skilled labor is needed to plan, build, and program the AI and wire it to the robots. We might even need substantial energy from fossil fuels to build such a plant. After the completion of the first plant, the army of robots used for that will be able to replicate additional solar energy power plants in other designated locations by themselves.

There will be no further need to start the process from scratch or enlist human talent to design or redesign new blueprints or drawings. In fact, no skill transfer will be needed, period. All the information fed into the robots during the first power plant would be reused for subsequent plants, except perhaps for some information about the topography of the new sites that can be easily learned by the AI system. A solar business can be fully automated with this approach.

Imagine competing businesses that could replicate such an army of robots continuously. Within a short time we could end up with thousands of solar power plants all built and managed by AI. The current fossil fuel dependent businesses would inevitably switch over to solar. Most Arabian countries that are rich in fossil fuels are rich in the desert sun too. All they need to do is just to switch from one technology to the other, and they have already started that process, with experts estimating many oil-rich countries will run out of their current oil reserves by 2040 at the latest. The transition to solar might happen well before that.

As the technology behind solar cells becomes ever more sophisticated with AI-aided research and as AI builds bigger and better power plants at a much lower cost, solar energy will be highly affordable. It will be the cheapest we have ever paid for such a bountiful, reliable, renewable energy supply. If AI is fully exploited to build a massive solar industry, within decades, like ants building their colonies or bees building honeycombs, without any human intervention solar plants will proliferate all over the globe.

There will be a glut of new entrepreneurial opportunities and plenty of high-tech jobs globally to support his massive solar power generation. Sadly there would be job losses too, as fossil industry begins to fold. Millions of jobs will be lost in the fossil fuel industry, and millions of jobs will be created in the solar power industry. We will witness a grand shift in jobs and careers.

Let's deep dive to envision how cheap energy could create abundance. Cost of any product essentially depends on three resources—energy, raw-materials, and labor. When energy becomes cheap, the mining cost which primarily depends on energy will plummet. With cheap energy and low-cost raw materials, the products will be very affordable. This invariably puts pressure on labor and eventually the low-skilled manual labor will be callously replaced by AI-driven versatile robots, making the products cheapest ever.

Consumers will be buying as never before as the prices are low. With AI-driven machines, manufacturing will be smart driving further innovation.

Today the patenting, prototyping, manufacturing, marketing, and warehousing that comes with bringing a new product to market is a high-risk venture. Because of these risks, many inventions from ordinary folks never saw the light of the day. They just died with the inventors. However, the story will be entirely different in the future. The smart AI manufacturing will engender a new breed of innovators bringing many great products and services to life. Our luxurious lives will be more luxurious. Life can't be any better.

With an inordinate level of abundance, the social responsibility of supporting the unemployed who have lost their jobs to the AI will not be a burden.

Easier Said Than Done

The grand vision of autonomously building solar plants is a Herculean task. Let's look at the realities of such a dream. The upfront costs are very high as are the financial risks. A typical industrial robot with the latest application-specific bells and whistles costs between US$80,000 and US$100,000. To program these robots, wire them up to an AI brain, and then train the AI to maneuver these machines and configure the whole system to autonomously build the solar power plant needs a massive team of programmers, engineers, and technicians to make it happen. It is truly a paradigm shift in the world of automation both in terms of planning and implementation.

The most difficult task in this endeavor is estimating the risks involved while treading unknown territory followed by securing financing for a highest-priced, experimental initiative such as building a fleet of automated machines to build solar complexes. Certainly it will be dependent on private investors, not governments, and even then who will be willing to step forward?

To make such a plan economically feasible, I believe there is only one answer: off-the-shelf, intelligent robotic systems that are prebuilt, prewired to AI, and preprogrammed with cognitive ability would make such a venture economically feasible.

The great news is, global manufacturing is moving towards such a digital revolution, called Industry 4.0. Industry 4.0 is commonly referred to as the fourth industrial revolution. As you will recall from history textbooks, the first industrial revolution was driven by steam power. The second industrial revolution was all about mass production using assembly lines, and the third industrial revolution was molded by the Internet and information technology. The fourth industrial revolution is being heavily influenced by AI and digital manufacturing. This includes smart systems such as robotics, IoT, cloud computing, and cognitive computing.

The driving force behind the emergence of such a digital movement in manufacturing is global competition. New products, new ideas, and new technologies are constantly hitting the market. Latest technologies like augmented reality, virtual reality, machine learning, and mobile computing are growing faster with big data. All these new technologies are forcing the manufacturing industry to move towards Industry 4.0 to survive the competition.

In today's solar power industry most onsite assembly projects are still manual as smart, versatile multitasking robots are not there yet. This is what we need in the solar industry. Fortunately this is what Industry 4.0 is desperately trying to unbox for the manufacturing industry in general, and the solar industry would be greatly benefitted by these versatile machines as well.

Event organizers around the world realize that Industry 4.0 is becoming mainstream, and there are multiple Industry 4.0 conferences and symposiums for many specialties happening every year around the world.

How fast Industry 4.0 brings intelligent systems to the marketplace will decide the pace of automation in the solar industry. The pace will be much faster if global think tanks can draw a distinctive relationship between Industry 4.0 and UBI, so there will be a conscious effort to speed up this process. Colleges and universities will have an equally responsible role to sync up their existing curriculum, with the latest cutting-edge technologies as and when they come out of the research rooms into the market, so the college grads will bolster the Industry 4.0 workforce.

Fossil Mess to Solar Mess

Although the world is desperate to replace fossil fuels, whether solar energy is the right substitute for the fast-growing economy of the future is worth exploring. Solar energy is surely green energy; however, it will inflict its own green damage to the ecosystem. Here is a quick glimpse into noxious pitfalls we might fall into as the world attempts to replace fossil fuels with solar.

It is estimated that when the entire fossil fuel industry is replaced by solar power, globally the land area used by solar power plants will catapult to about 120,000 square km (46,332 square miles), nearly half the size of Arizona, which will have its own environmental impact. The other bad news is that solar power generation is not efficient during winter. For example, in Germany the installed solar power is about 30 GW. News reports state that it has captured about 50 percent of the national power supply. That is true—but only in summer. In winter it only generates about 10 percent of its capacity. So in such places the solar power plants must be many times bigger to make up for the winter shortage. If we extrapolate this to all cities in colder regions, the land usage would be much bigger than what we computed above. The large-scale land usage will have a detrimental environmental impact. That problem could be offset to some extent by having wind turbines built in conjunction with the solar farms to generate power during winter. That reduces the size of land to some degree.

Installing a wind turbine is less complicated than solar panels because the entire wind turbine can be mass produced in a factory using robots and autonomously transported and installed in high-wind zones.

However, wind-powered energy generation is not as steady as solar powered energy; wind speed fluctuates by season and even by time of day. Obviously these wind and solar power plants need excess capacity to supply power adequately. That means the land area that is estimated above would shoot up many-fold in cold climates.

The other challenge is that oversized wind-solar power plants apparently produce surplus energy in summer that may not be needed, causing some shifts in the economy. If power becomes much cheaper in the summer, industries might start producing more goods during summer and less during winter. Then entire industries will start building around seasonal energy availability.

Additionally, as battery technology improves, people will buy batteries and store cheap energy during summer and use it in winter. This economic shift poses new challenges to the power plant industry in terms of financing, risk estimation, and the environmental impact of battery waste. We will see many such unique non-green impacts on the economy as we move more away from fossil fuels and toward solar and wind energy.

The greatest non-green impact of cheap energy comes in the form of exponential production of goods. With cheap energy the world will consume goods like never before. The production of goods will be exponential and so will the raw-material demand. Underground mining will be rampant to satisfy the hungry market and to build solar plants and wind turbines. Not only will substantial land be appropriated by these power plants, but the earth will also be increasingly mined and burrowed unscrupulously year after year. If the economy grows by say 5 percent each year, so will the land sizes of solar/wind power plants. We'll be moving from a fossil fuel mess to a solar mess.

This potential calamity must force us to develop innovative technologies to produce energy that is truly green: carbon-free, radiation-free, and compact using less land area. Here is a quick peek at the latest global endeavors that are already working to find that true green energy.

Commonwealth Fusion Systems, a private company, in collaboration with MIT is attempting to produce clean, abundant energy via fusion technology (not the fission technology used in nuclear reactors). Using a new class of high-temperature superconductors and ultra-powerful magnets, they are able to regulate fusion reaction to smash hydrogen atoms together giving off helium and huge amounts of energy without nuclear waste.

Similarly, scientists in France are attempting to generate power with fusion technology. The International Thermonuclear Experimental Reactor (ITER), a massive tokamak fusion reactor, is under construction in France with an investment of $14 billion dollars from countries like United States, Russia, China, India, Japan, and South Korea. The scientists are hoping to generate power by 2025.

The US Department of Energy's (DOE) Princeton Plasma Physics Laboratory (PPPL) is also involved in studying tokamak experiments.

Scientists in the UK are also working on nuclear fusion. Atkins is partnering with Tokamak Energy to generate the first electricity by 2025.

Fusion holds the most promising clean and renewable energy worldwide. It has no radioactive waste and is a great alternative to the land grabbing wind and solar power plants.

However, we should be cautious about cheap, abundant energy and not chop the branch we're standing on. Generating cheap energy and creating excessive abundance in society may lead to destroying our planet as we mine it to our hearts' content to satisfy the accompanying exponential industrial growth. The potential environmental impact of mining is mind-boggling. Underground mining causes soil erosion, development of unstable land with sinkholes, earthquakes, loss of biodiversity, groundwater contamination by chemicals leading to health problems, and so on.

But we are decades away from these catastrophic consequences of cheap, abundant energy, so we must consider looking at deep space voyages to mine on asteroid belt instead of on Earth in the future.

Although it is too futuristic an idea, it is not untimely to have a glimpse into the world of asteroids to enumerate alternative resources. An asteroid belt is a region of space between the orbits of Mars and Jupiter where millions of asteroids orbit the Sun. The asteroid belt contains millions of asteroids, and they come in a variety of sizes from as small as less than a mile across to as large as one-quarter the size of our moon. Some metallic asteroids contain a rich mixture of gold, platinum, nickel, magnesium, iridium, palladium, and other precious metals such as rhodium, osmium, and ruthenium.

The main challenge of asteroid mining is the distance. Mining will be extremely expensive with today's technology, so not many have paid much attention to this futuristic option. However, as we move into the fusion era and an autonomous robotic world, asteroid mining—and space exploration in general—are researched in greater detail.

At some point in the future, as we empower ourselves with true green alternatives like fusion energy, we should plan on winding up the solar mess that we have created here on earth. We must conceptualize our dexterity to protect the planet and keep it safe.

Solar power is only a stepping stone to go beyond fossil fuels; it's not the end game. It will ultimately be atomic energy sources like fusion reactors that take us to the next era of technological evolution.

Although the future looks bright, for now we should focus on coming out of the current fossil fuel mess we have concocted. Industry 4.0 is giving the world strong wings to fly into that amazing future. We should build solar and wind power plants as much and as fast as we can until we replace fossil fuels entirely.

I hope this discussion makes us contemplate beyond unemployment and beyond cheap energy. We need to protect the planet from unconscionable mining that is bound to happen because of cheap energy.

Epilogue

Wisely Employed

Employment is a recent phenomenon and so is unemployment. Before industrialization most of the world's population lived in villages, and every household had a farm and domesticated animals to support their livelihood. Each household was self-sufficient in terms of food and shelter, although many creature comforts were missing. Life was hard but no desperate dependency on jobs. There was no concept of career per se.

Only after industrialization, did we produce goods of value and started depending on them for comfort and luxury. To enjoy the urban lifestyle did we educate ourselves and formulated careers and moved away from those agri-lifestyles. Just imagine fetching drinking water from the river every day. There is no turning back. Urban life has come a long way. Although many villages in remote regions still live in those times. But the urban population has moved on.

Employment allowed us to enjoy an urban lifestyle and along with it came the stress of maintaining the skillset. Unemployment is always right behind employment. When our skills don't fit the bill, we are not employable anymore.

Now we are at the threshold of inventing machines that can do most of our manual jobs. Does it mean that we can afford to be unemployable in the future and do nothing and getting everything done by the machines?

Never mind bothering who would build and manage those machines. What if we develop machines that can look after themselves and replicate as needed, just like the way we get free honey from honey bees who work without any human intervention and reproduce and maintain themselves? Then yes there is a possibility.

Such a possibility comes with a hefty price though. Remember our planet created intelligence too. Plants and animals have their own genetic intelligence. There was no self-thinking, self-learning intelligence on the planet until we came along. We are the AGI our planet produced. We are the self-aware and self-evolving species of mother earth. We almost destroyed the planet, till earth showed its ugly face of global warming. We haven't stopped yet; we are still digging and burrowing. We will continue to do so to support the global economy. We can't stop digging the planet unless we bring the global economy to a screeching halt, which we don't.

The AGI that we are planning to build is much more powerful than we humans. Its processing power will be zillion times that of humans, limited only by the design. It means that the AGI that we are planning will do exactly the same to Earth as we did but at a much larger scale.

We can't let such an intelligence to evolve without supervision. We have a responsible job at hand to strategize what kind of AGI we can afford to build. AGI will certainly do all manual tasks and make our life luxurious, but its ability can't be unlimited. We have to develop machines that play by our rules, protecting our species.

What if, intentionally or unintentionally, we develop a rogue AGI and the genie gets out of the bottle? The first thing that this superintelligence does is, it will use planetary resources to evolve. This is similar to what we are doing now at a smaller scale. We are digging planet earth to build rockets to terraform nearby planets. We already have plans to colonize the moon and Mars. SpaceX already has plans to take the first human to space by 2023. AGI that we are planning to build will be no different. With unlimited intelligence and unlimited competence to explore, it may destroy our planet for resources. It may not kill us, as we are too small a threat, but it may destroy planet earth for resources.

In the future, can the world afford to be unemployed, laze around in beaches and let the machines replicate? Hell no. If we let the machines evolve on their own, we are invariably inviting exponential threat. We have to nurture AI strategically. On its journey towards AGI, it is bound to create a new breed of machines and a new breed of skills much different than we have now. It is wise to prepare for those eventualities.

Acknowledgments

Grateful acknowledgment is made many international organizations having provided useful quality information for public research. They include organizations like World Health Organization, National Center for Public Policy and Higher Education, www.house.gov, www.cbo.gov, www.eia.doe.gov, www.nasa.gov, www.ers.usda.gov, stanford.edu, forbes.com, ibm.com, dhs.gov, industry40summit.com, darpa.mil, epa.gov, nature.org, and www.cms.gov.

There are several groups of people to whom I am very thankful for their help and advice. Many thanks to reviewers including *Kirkus Reviews, Clarion Reviews,* and Kathleen Tracy for her valuable advice and feedback. And thanks to my family and friends for their helpful comments, advice, and support.

Bibliography

"Aerosols and Incoming Sunlight (Direct Effects)." NASA Observatory. November 2, 2010. https://earthobservatory.nasa.gov/Features/Aerosols/page3.php

"Artificial Intelligence Replaces Physicists." The Australian National University. Last modified May 16, 2016. http://www.anu.edu.au/news/all-news/artificial-intelligence-replaces-physicists

"Artificial Intelligence Takes on the Stock Market." BBC (video). 01:21. February 10, 2016. http://www.bbc.com/news/av/technology-35405336/artificial-intelligence-takes-on-the-stock-market

"Artificial Intelligence." Wikipedia. Accessed July 12, 2018. https://en.wikipedia.org/wiki/Artificial_intelligence

"Atmospheric Aerosols: What Are They, and Why Are They So Important?" Bob Allen (ed.). NASA. Last modified August 7, 2017.

https://www.nasa.gov/centers/langley/n
ews/factsheets/Aerosols.html

Baker, David R. "Robots Cut Solar Construction
Costs." *San Francisco Chronicle*. June 17,
2013.
https://www.sfchronicle.com/business/a
rticle/Robots-cut-solar-construction-
costs-4604343.php

"Beijing Uses Machine Learning and Big Data to
Target Pollution Controls." Apolitical.
Accessed July 12, 2018.
https://apolitical.co/solution_article/beiji
ng-uses-machine-learning-big-data-target-
pollution-controls/

Bohannon, John. "A New Breed of Scientist, with
Brains of Silicon." *Science*. July 5, 2017.
http://www.sciencemag.org/news/2017/
07/new-breed-scientist-brains-silicon

Callaghan, Greg. "Can Swarms of Seed-Bearing
Drones Help Regrow the Planet's
Forests?" *Sydney Morning Herald*. August
26, 2017.
https://www.smh.com.au/lifestyle/can-
swarms-of-seedbearing-drones-help-
regrow-the-planets-forests-20170823-
gy2ei5.html

"Carbon Capture and Storage." ExxonMobil.
Accessed July 12, 2018.

http://corporate.exxonmobil.com/en/tec hnology/carbon-capture-and-storage

"Carbon Capture and Storage." Wikipedia. Accessed July 13, 2018. https://en.wikipedia.org/wiki/Carbon_ca pture_and_storage

"Carbon Capture and the Future of Coal Power." NRG. Accessed July 12, 2018, https://www.nrg.com/case-studies/petra-nova.html

"Carbon Dioxide 101." National Energy Technology Laboratory. Accessed July 13, 2018. https://www.netl.doe.gov/research/coal/carbon-storage/carbon-storage-faqs/what-are-the-primary-sources-of-co2

"Carbon Dioxide in Earth's Atmosphere." Wikipedia. Accessed July 13, 2018. https://en.wikipedia.org/wiki/Carbon_di oxide_in_Earth%27s_atmosphere

"Carbon Footprint Calculator." Environmental Protection Agency. Accessed July 13, 2018. https://www3.epa.gov/carbon-footprint-calculator/

"Carbon Sequestration." Lamont-Doherty Earth Observatory. Accessed July 12, 2018. http://www.ldeo.columbia.edu/gpg/proj ects/carbon-sequestration

"Carbon Sink." Wikipedia. Accessed July 13,
    2018.
    https://en.wikipedia.org/wiki/Carbon_si
    nk

Clark, Jen. "What Is the Internet of Things?"
    Internet of Things Blog. November 17, 2016.
    https://www.ibm.com/blogs/Internet-of-
    things/what-is-the-iot/

Conway, Erik. "What's in a Name? Global
    Warming vs. Climate Change Global."
    NASA. Accessed July 12, 2018.
    https://www.nasa.gov/topics/earth/featu
    res/climate_by_any_other_name.html

"DARPA Robotics Challenge (DRC) (Archived)."
    Defense Advanced Research Projects
    Agency. Accessed July 13, 2018.
    https://www.darpa.mil/program/darpa-
    robotics-challenge

"Deep Convective Clouds and Chemistry
    Experiment (DC3)." The National Center
    for Atmospheric Research. Accessed July
    12, 2018.
    https://www2.acom.ucar.edu/dc3

"Deep Thunder Now Hyper-Local on a Global
    Scale." IBM (blog). June 15, 2016.
    https://www.ibm.com/blogs/research/2
    016/06/deep-thunder-now-hyper-local-
    global/

"eMotion Butterflies." Festo. Accessed July 13, 2018.
https://www.festo.com/group/en/cms/1 0216.htm

"Global Climate Change: Vital Signs of the Planet." NASA. Accessed July 13, 2018. https://climate.nasa.gov/vital-signs/carbon-dioxide/

Hansen, James, Makiko Sato, Pushker Kharecha, and Karina von Schuckmann "Earth's Energy Imbalance." NASA Goddard Institute for Space Studies. January 2012. https://www.giss.nasa.gov/research/brief s/hansen_16/

http://carbonengineering.com/

http://www.predpol.com/

http://www.shotspotter.com/

https://globalthermostat.com/

https://stanleyinnovation.com

https://us.hikvision.com/en

https://www.ibm.com

https://www.industry40summit.com/2018-programme/

https://www.kavout.com/

https://www.nature.org/greenliving/carboncalcul ator/index.htm

https://www.research.ibm.com/green-horizons/interactive

https://www.transcriptic.com/ "Internet of Things." Wikipedia. Accessed July 12, 2018. https://en.wikipedia.org/wiki/Internet_of_things

"IPCC Fourth Assessment Report: Climate Change 2007." Intergovernmental Panel on Climate Change. Accessed July 13, 2018. https://www.ipcc.ch/publications_and_data/ar4/wg1/en/ch7s7-3-2-2.html

Kumar, Vijay. "The Future of Flying Objects." Ted Talks (video). 13:10. April 2015. https://www.ted.com/talks/vijay_kumar_the_future_of_flying_robots

Mahtanim, Shibani and Zusha Elinson. "Artificial Intelligence Could Soon Enhance Real-Time Police Surveillance." *Wall Street Journal.* Last modified April 3, 2018. https://www.wsj.com/articles/artificial-intelligence-could-soon-enhance-real-time-police-surveillance-1522761813

Marr, Bernard. "What Is the Difference Between Artificial Intelligence and Machine Learning?" *Forbes.* December 6, 2016. https://www.forbes.com

McCarthy, John. "What Is AI?/Basic Questions." Accessed July 12, 2018.

http://jmc.stanford.edu/artificial-
intelligence/what-is-ai/index.html

"NOAA to Develop New Global Weather
Model." National Oceanic and
Atmospheric Administration. July 27,
2016. http://www.noaa.gov/media-
release/noaa-to-develop-new-global-
weather-model

O'Reilly, Lara. "A Japanese Ad Agency Invented
an AI Creative Director—and Ad Execs
Preferred Its Ad to a Human's." *Business
Insider.* March 12, 2917.
http://www.businessinsider.com/mccann
-japans-ai-creative-director-creates-better-
ads-than-a-human-2017-3

"Quest Carbon Capture and Storage." Shell
Canada. Accessed July 12, 2018.
https://www.shell.ca/en_ca/about-
us/projects-and-sites/quest-carbon-
capture-and-storage-project.html

"Radio Frequency Identification (RFID): What Is
It?" Department of Homeland Security.
Last modified July 6, 2009.
https://www.dhs.gov/radio-frequency-
identification-rfid-what-it

"Radio-Frequency Identification." Wikipedia.
Accessed July 12, 2018.

https://en.wikipedia.org/wiki/Radio-frequency_identification

"Safely Storing Carbon Dioxide." Chevron. Accessed July 12, 2018. https://www.chevron.com/stories/safely-storing-co2

Shaw, Darren. "How Wimbledon Is Using IBM Watson AI to Power Highlights, Analytics, and Enriched Fan Experiences." IBM. July 6, 2017. https://www.ibm.com/blogs/watson/2017/07/ibm-watsons-ai-is-powering-wimbledon-highlights-analytics-and-a-fan-experiences/

Smith, John R. "IBM Research Takes Watson to Hollywood with the First Cognitive Movie Trailer." *IBM Think* (blog). August 31, 2016. https://www.ibm.com/blogs/think/2016/08/cognitive-movie-trailer/

"Solar Radiation Management." Wikipedia. Accessed July 13, 2018. https://en.wikipedia.org/wiki/Solar_radiation_management

"Sophia." Hanson Robotics. Accessed July 12, 2018. http://www.hansonrobotics.com/robot/sophia/

"The New Carbon Economy." CO2 Solutions. Accessed July 12, 2018. https://www.co2solutions.com/

"Tomra's Mineral and Ore Sorting Equipment for More Profit." Tomra. Accessed July 13, 2018. https://www.tomra.com/en/sorting/mining

"Trends in Atmospheric Carbon Dioxide." Earth System Research Laboratory. Accessed July 13, 2018. https://www.esrl.noaa.gov/gmd/ccgg/trends/gl_data.html

Walker, Jon. "Chatbot Comparison: Facebook, Microsoft, Amazon, and Google." *Telemergence*. March 29, 2018. https://www.techemergence.com/chatbot-comparison-facebook-microsoft-amazon-google/

"What Is Carbon Dioxide Removal and Why Is It Important?" Climeworks. Accessed July 12, 2018. http://www.climeworks.com/co2-removal/

"What is CCS?" Carbon Capture and Storage Association. Accessed July 13, 2018.http://www.ccsassociation.org/what-is-ccs/

"What Is SRM?" Solar Radiation Management
Governance Initiative. Accessed July 13,
2018. http://www.srmgi.org/what-is-srm

Index

3

A